STUFF PARISIANS LIKE

100%
PARISIEN
APPROUVÉ

STUFF PARISIANS LIKE

Olivier Magny

BERKLEY BOOKS • NEW YORK

THE BERKLEY PUBLISHING GROUP
Published by the Penguin Group
Penguin Group (USA) Inc.
375 Hudson Street, New York, New York 10014, USA
Penguin Group (Canada), 90 Eglinton Avenue East, Suite 700, Toronto, Ontario M4P 2Y3, Canada (a division of Pearson Penguin Canada Inc.)
Penguin Books Ltd., 80 Strand, London WC2R 0RL, England
Penguin Group Ireland, 25 St. Stephen's Green, Dublin 2, Ireland (a division of Penguin Books Ltd.)
Penguin Group (Australia), 250 Camberwell Road, Camberwell, Victoria 3124, Australia (a division of Pearson Australia Group Pty. Ltd.)
Penguin Books India Pvt. Ltd., 11 Community Centre, Panchsheel Park, New Delhi—110 017, India
Penguin Group (NZ), 67 Apollo Drive, Rosedale, Auckland 0632, New Zealand (a division of Pearson New Zealand Ltd.)
Penguin Books (South Africa) (Pty.) Ltd., 24 Sturdee Avenue, Rosebank, Johannesburg 2196, South Africa

Penguin Books Ltd., Registered Offices: 80 Strand, London WC2R 0RL, England

Interior photos by Olivier Magny
Cover design by Annette Fiore Defex
Cover art by John Jay
Book design by Pauline Neuwirth

PRINTING HISTORY
Berkley trade paperback edition / July 2011

Library of Congress Cataloging-in-Publication Data

Magny, Olivier.
Stuff Parisians like : discovering the quoi in the je ne sais quoi / Olivier Magny.—1st ed.
p. cm.
ISBN 978-0-425-24118-9

1. Paris (France—Civilization—21st century—Humor. 2. Paris (France— Social life and customs—Humor. 3. National characteristics, French—Humor. I. Title.
DC715M317 2011
944'.36100207—dc22

2010049192

PRINTED IN THE UNITED STATES OF AMERICA

10 9 8 7 6 5 4 3 2 1

Acknowledgments

This book would never have existed without the lenience of Nicolas Paradis, my business partner at Ô Chateau. All the time I spent writing *Stuff Parisians Like*, I did not spend working on Ô Chateau.

He's quite the business partner; I'm well aware of it. No matter what the name on the cover says, this book is also vastly his.

Other special thanks go to the readers of my blog. If it wasn't for their kind words month after month, I would never have kept on with my silly writing.

So merci, really.

(Here, the first French myth debunked: Not all Frenchies are ungrateful pricks. . . . More in the following pages, stick with me).

Introduction

In my broken English, I've written every word of this book.

Except for 6.

That is "Discovering the *quoi* in the *je-ne-sais-quoi*." I must say I'm somewhat bummed for I think this is the wittiest line of the book, the most efficient, too.

I'm accountable for the other less witty, less efficient lines in here.

English

Parisians know English very well.

Usually better than French.

English words have become a necessary ornament to the French spoken in Paris.

The Parisian talks about *son spirit, son timing*, or *son management* with his friends. *Il squeeze, il checke, il switche.* Parisians working in the corporate world are the best at English. They fully master it. All day, they deal with "meetings," "slides," "open space," and "feedback."

Their nine-to-five lingo soon enough turns into a second nature: the Parisian *est corporate.* Thank God for the corporate world. The Parisian knows that French has its limits. What in the world could be a translation for *spirit* anyway?

When a Parisian shares that *il est en speed car il a squeezé un gros meeting entre un lunch avec son boss et un conf call avec son CEO* ("he is late because he scheduled a big meeting between a lunch with his boss and a conference call with the CEO"), he is completely oblivious to the fact that his French is somewhat sprinkled with English words. That's what knowledge does to you. Knoweldge acquired in the workplace, while traveling, or in magazines. With most of the press headquartered in Paris, new fashion, people, or shopping sections flourish in every publication.

To the Parisian, English is secretly more cool and quite obviously much simpler than French. And is a fantastic way for the Parisian to recognize his peers. While all Parisians will understand the sentence above at once, only a few *provinciaux* will. Most will somehow mock the Parisian for talking like this. That's what ignorance does to you.

Faced with criticism, Parisians may react in two opposite fashions. Some will admit: *Ouais, je sais, c'est grave, hein, j'peux pas m'empêcher, c'est con, hein?!* ("Yes, I know, I can't stop myself. It's stupid, right?") Others will strike back: *Oh la la, évolue un peu, c'est bon, faut pas être passéiste comme ça: Relax, Max.* ("Suck it up, it's all good and you don't have to live in the past like that all the time: Relax.")

The Parisian is the victim of his own knowledge. *Vraiment, c'est hard d'être Parisien.*

USEFUL TIP: If you're a native Anglophone, first learn about the meaning Parisians have put behind each English word. Surprises may occur.

SOUND LIKE A PARISIAN: *Non, mais le deal c'est qu'y'a pas de guest list, c'est tout!* ("No, the deal is that there is no guest list, end of the story.")

South America

Parisians love South America. There is no exception to that rule.

The definition of South America for Parisians is simple: South America is anything south of America. The existence of Central America is not a relevant question in Paris. The actual existence of several countries within South America is already bewildering enough. All Parisians know that South America is colorful, authentic, and happy. Very little differentiation ought to be made between Guatemala and Peru.

During his student years, a Parisian customarily takes a trip to South America. *A l'aventure.* Going to South America without a backpack would be considered very poor travel standards to a Parisian. One is to backpack in South America. Backpacking for the Parisian includes traveling with a backpack and *des bonnes chaussures de marche.* And sleeping in hotels.

Returning from a trip to South America, the Parisian will systematically say it was *génial.* He will have a word about *les couleurs.* And *les gens.* Though, obviously, it was *un peu roots.* For sure, it was.

Most Parisians have a friend from South America. Those who don't wished they did. South American friends bring lightheartedness and a Spanish accent to Parisian parties. These are key to a good party. Lightheartedness is a quality

Parisians love in people from South America and Belgium. They admire it in English people. And they despise it in people from France or the U.S.

The only negative point Parisians sometimes mention about South America is *la violence.* Parisians all have a friend who got mugged in Brazil. Yet Parisians' love for South America is here to stay. For, ultimately, the Parisian love for South America is a typical form of Parisian love, made of an authentic appreciation for qualities the Parisian wished he had and a comfortable feeling of insuperable superiority over the subject of his love.

USEFUL TIP: Go to Argentina.

SOUND LIKE A PARISIAN: *J'ai trop envie de me faire un voyage en Amérique du Sud.* ("I so want to take a trip to South America.")

Robert Doisneau

Parisians like Paris. And they like to display that they do.

Posters are the Parisians' vector of choice to celebrate their affection for their city.

Putting up a poster of a Parisian monument would be such an outsider's thing to do (though some lazy Parisians will opt for the series of pictures related to the construction of the Eiffel Tower). The whole Aristide Bruant thing has been over for fifteen years.

These days, a real Parisian prefers to put up on his wall, on his fridge, or in his *toilettes* a picture of Robert Doisneau. Robert Doisneau's mid-twentieth century black-and-white pictures usually represent Parisians (lovers or children) in Paris. Doisneau's pictures give to a room a gloomy/melancholic/artistic touch that Parisians cannot get enough of. The Paris represented in these photographs is the romantic, eternal, and *populaire* Paris. As Doisneau liked to say, *"Ma photo, c'est le monde tel que je souhaite qu'il soit"* ("My photo, it's how I wish the world would be"). Parisians understand this very well. They, too, would like the world to be black and white, charming and melancholic.

As for all mainstream things in Paris, an implicit social classification exists. What you display on your walls defines where you stand socially. Where you stand socially defines what you display on your walls. The bottom of the Doisneau hierarchy is evidently his most well-known photograph, *Le Baiser de l'Hôtel de Ville.* All teenage Parisian girls own a reproduction of this picture. Adults putting up a poster of *Le Baiser de l'Hotel de Ville* send the clear message that either they have stuck to the teenage-girl level or that they are unaware of existing social codes in Paris. Both lead to sheer ridicule and diminished social credit.

Which Doisneau picture the Parisian chooses to display in his home will help the visitor conjure up a finer portrait of his host. Aspiring artists will cherish *Les Pains de Picasso,* freethinkers will opt for *Les frères, rue du Docteur Lecène,* smiley *carabins* for *Regard Obique,* while school nostalgia is clearly displayed in *L'information scolaire, école rue Buffon.* A *photo de Doisneau* in a Parisian apartment is like a status update on a Facebook profile: a key to one's identity.

Parisian women have a special liking for Robert Doisneau, but Parisian men are happy to cope with his artwork. Should conflicts appear about the relevance to display a Doisneau photograph on a wall, a typical Parisian trade-off is to opt for a Doisneau coffee table book. Always a great hit when you have friends over. Flipping through the pages of the book, other Parisians will sit back on the couch, look at the pictures together, and simply say, *"J'l'adore celle-là, elle est trop bien."*

More than just Doisneau, Parisians know their arts.

USEFUL TIP: Impress your friends by knowing another photographer besides Robert Doisneau.

SOUND LIKE A PARISIAN: *J'adooore Doisneau.*

Calling People *Beaufs*

Le beauf (pronounce "bohf") is somewhere between the American redneck and the English pikey. In French imagery, *le beauf* drinks beer, wears wifebeaters, watches soccer endlessly, and vacations in his RV.

In Paris, the definition is a bit broader.

For the Parisian, every person he does not know is a *beauf.*

Calling people *beaufs* is a wonderful thing for Parisians. It allows them to assert conveniently their superiority while not going through the trouble of enduring a painstaking analysis that might lead them to interrogations about themselves or others. Indeed, the *beauf* verdict is an immediate one. Some *beaufs* are pushing it and Parisians won't get much credit for pointing them out: "White socks? *Quel beauf!*"

Too easy.

Superior perceived social status is acquired by mocking habits and attitudes that are typical of upper-class or even better—rich—people. "He's spending the weekend in Deauville? Can't believe it. *Quel beauf!*" "Is he really driving a Hummer? *Quel gros beauf!*" By striking his audience with an unsuspected *beauf* designation, the Parisian scores serious social points: "Did he really take his nephew to Disneyland? *Quel beauf!*" The ultimate goal is to make all the people surrounding the Parisian wonder if, compared to him, they are not ultimately complete *beaufs.*

It is Parisian wisdom that one is always someone else's *beauf.* Yet the Parisian can never tolerate the threatening shadow of *beaufitude* upon his head. When one of the things he says, wears, or does gets him called a *beauf* by one of his fellow Parisians (who else?), disdain is the appropriate answer. By disdainfully calling on self-derision or edginess, the Parisian not only washes off the attack but also pours the *beaufitude* back onto his initial offender.

The beauty of living in Paris is that *beauf* is a concept applicable to nonhuman things: destinations, activities, pieces of clothing, music, decoration, books . . . Almost all things can be *beauf* in Paris. . . .

. . . thus making Parisians feel good about themselves in all situations.

USEFUL TIP: At a costume party, amuse your Parisian friends by opting for a *beauf* costume.

SOUND LIKE A PARISIAN: *C'est vraiment des gros beaufs ces Américains. . . .*

Wedding Days

Parisians have mixed feelings about weddings.

When Parisians first hear about a wedding, they get excited. Automatically. Not by the good news itself, but by the announcement of it: *le faire-part.* This one piece of paper that defines both the class origin of the couple and the social value of the new household. *Le faire-part* is an indelible imprint. Friends will find it *super classique, hyper moche*, or *original, disons. Le faire-part* is not really a wedding announcement note. It's more one of these bound-to-fail tests. Automatically, indeed, excitement ensues for the Parisian.

Such pace is hard to sustain. At this point then, the Parisian gets annoyed with the wedding. He happily claims that he does not want to attend. Fun events are by essence painful to the Parisian. When fun takes the form of a social obligation, the Parisian sees nothing but nonsense. But he will give in. Resiliently for the Parisian man, in vague hysterical stress for the Parisian woman: *Oh la la, j'ai rien à me mettre. Et puis j'suis grosse, faut absolument que je perde cinq kilos d'ici le mariage.* ("I have nothing to wear. Plus I'm fat. I absolutely must lose ten pounds before this wedding.")

Then comes the glory day. Every time, the same magic happens. The nice dresses, the charming church, the *beauf* uncle . . . Parisians smile. Genuinely. They are happy to be there. For a few minutes. And, slowly but surely, the soothing pleasure that comes with the reassuring ceremonies of life gives way to a new form of excitement. A more Parisian form of excitement that comes with the unconscious treat of encapsulating countless new people and groups into little boxes. Plenty of tiny boxes—usually sealed for life. The excitement is all the greater as all these people are acquaintances of a friend or a family member. *Oh, putain, tu l'as vu avec sa cravate l'autre, oh la la, putain, c'est pas possible.* ("Oh, *putain,* check out that guy—can't believe the tie he's wearing.") It is impossible to have more fun than this.

But a good Parisian wedding also allows Parisian guests to judge while enjoying: the ceremony, the venue, the looks of the guests, the food served. This happens during dinner. Good things come to those who wait.

The past few years have seen an escalation in the broad category of *les discours.* Between each course, one, two, or three *discours.* Every time, the same interrogations flourish around the tables: *Alors c'est qui ca? Ah, les amis d'ecole? Il a fait l'ESSEC, lui, c'est ca? Bon, bah ca devrait etre pas mal alors!* ("Who are these guys? Oh, friends from grad school? Well, should be quite good then!") Just like in Roman times, each conversation has only two possible outcomes. One, guests are captivated, smile, laugh, or are touched. Two, *discours* sucks: polite guests simply look down; cheeky ones look for partners in crime to makes faces at.

An advanced form of *discours* is one enriched with a PowerPoint presentation presenting old and funny pictures of the couple. Pictures are certainly powerful allies to the uninspired. But the climax of the *discours de mariage* is *la chanson.* Cousins, friends from college, colleagues . . . Each coherent group feels a disturbing obligation to come up with a personalized cover of a famous song dedicated to the newlyweds. While some of these songs confine to comic genius, most navigate somewhere between plainly useless and straight-up embarrassing. The moment when a group of friends grabs the microphone and says, *"Lili, Nico, on vous a préparé une p'tite chanson"* is the moment where Lili for the first time considers running away in the middle of dinner a worthy option.

The rest of the night is history. Older guests will go to bed early. College friends will get drunk and dance. The rare single friends left will regret the good old days where weddings were a good opportunity to meet people. The process will be debriefed and continued in small groups. Newlyweds will be amazed of how fast the day flew by.

The next day, everyone will agree that *Non, vraiment, c'était super.*

USEFUL TIP: When it comes to *discours*, "Go strong or go home" sounds likes a wise policy.

SOUND LIKE A PARISIAN: *Ecoute, finalement, c'était hyper sympa le mariage. Ca me saoulait un peu d'y aller, mais vraiment, super cool finalement. A part le DJ, ca, c'était un peu la cata, le reste vraiment, c'était super.* ("Listen, in the end, it was a great wedding. I sorta didn't want to go, but really, it was cool in the end. Other than the DJ, who was a bit of a catastrophe, but really the rest was great.")

Le Caramel au Beurre Salé

Sweet in Paris is guilty. Gently guilty. Sugar carries all the afflictions of decadence. It is coating and fattening, sensual and tempting, enjoyable and slippery. Anything sweet in Paris should therefore be consumed in great moderation. Just enough for the threatening shadow of decadence not to ruin the tender moment of sweet collapse.

In that unspoken tug-of-war between good and bad, the Parisian found an ally in *le caramel au beurre salé. Le caramel au beurre salé* is as sweet as it gets. Devilishly so. But in all that sweetness and perversion comes a salvatory adjective, a redeeming flavor: *le salé.* Taunting and irreverent. Obedient and rebellious. *Le salé* makes *caramel* acceptable for the Parisian. It makes indulging almost enjoyable. Salt is one powerful little thing.

Le caramel au beurre salé was once a *bretonne* oddity. The uncanny account for the local tradition of salting butter. But its enchanting taste and redemptive qualities made it popular beyond its *bigounden* nest. Over the past few years, *le caramel au beurre salé* has become Parisians' white flag in their inner battle against guilty feelings. *Le caramel au beurre salé* is now to be found virtually in anything sweet: *la glace, les macarons, les bonbons* . . . But the Parisian's favorite expression of it is *le bonbon. Le p'tit bonbon.* Circumscribed indulgences are small apotheoses to the Parisian. This bonbon is an expert stroke. Expert strokes are something most Parisians end up counting exclusively on their pâtissier for.

When a Parisian reads *Caramel au beurre salé* on a dessert menu, he usually bursts with an irrepressible *"Oh, caramel au beurre salé . . ."* At this point, the odds for the Parisian to give in reach a peak. Salt miraculously washes sugar away, brushes off decadence. The Parisian is freed.

Amen.

USEFUL TIP: When it comes to *caramel au beurre salé*, Henri Le Roux is the man.

SOUND LIKE A PARISIAN: *C'était servi avec une boule de caramel au beurre salé . . . hyper bon! J'adore le caramel au beurre salé.* ("It came with a scoop of salted butter caramel ice cream . . . really good stuff. I love salted butter caramel.")

The Word *Sympa*

In the United States, one can get by with mastering only ten adjectives.

In Paris, one is enough.

Sympa, that is. *Sympa* is the most useful adjective in Paris. Initially, *sympa* is short for *sympathique. Sympa* is something that is nice. People, places, moments, activities can all be *sympa.* Being fantastically noncommittal, *sympa* grew to become a tremendously popular adjective. Not only can most things be *sympa* but they usually are. In Paris, there really is only one answer to the question *C'était comment?*

Sympa!

Using it extensively, Parisians managed to empty the word of its very substance: the way it is said gives it its actual meaning. To decipher what a Parisian really thinks of something or someone, it is key to be attentive to the tone of the *sympa* he will most likely come up with as an answer. Tone and facial expression. Only then will you know a bit more about what the Parisian really thinks.

Sympa became such a popular adjective in Paris because it sends out messages that the Parisian is happy to convey about himself. Because it's short for something, *sympa* is vaguely colloquial, making the Parisian seem vaguely laid back when using it. On top of this, *sympa* is a fantastic buffer against any form of enthusiasm. *Sympa* is nice but it is still very far from *excellent, génial, exceptionnel, formidable*, or *fantastique*. It is just *sympa*. By saying something or someone is *sympa*, the Parisian gives it a good point. But not too good of a point.

Thank God.

Parisians could not invent a better word even if they looked for it. *Sympa* is about the object. It is not about the person who says it. The object exhales. The Parisian is weirdly passive in judging something or someone as *sympa*. He becomes a mere receptacle for the world he lives in. This posture of passive humility is yet another reason for the popularity of the term. It says, "I judge without judging. Whatever I say, it is not my fault." Parisians these days love this tepid feeling of social innocence. Flamboyance is long gone.

Making *sympa* such a close companion, Parisians mechanically diminished the strength of its original meaning. Thus making phrases like *hyper sympa* or *super sympa* major hits. Among younger Parisians, the word *sympa* is so prevailing that its use deprived of *hyper, super, vraiment*, or *carrément* is suspicious.

If a young Parisian tells you that a place is *sympa*, he probably doesn't actually think much of it. With nothing but positive words, Parisian youth downgrades reality.

Beat that, youngsters from everywhere else....

USEFUL TIP: There is no connection whatsoever between *sympathique* in French and "sympathetic" in English. *Faux amis!*

SOUND LIKE A PARISIAN: *C'était sympa, mais je suis rentrée tôt, j'étais crevée.* ("It was *sympa*, but I came home early, I was exhausted.")

Sushi

There are three dimensions to being cool in Paris: owning an iPhone, wearing Converse shoes, and eating sushi—at least twice a week. Failing to fulfill one of these conditions will make the Parisian lame, old, and uncool.

Over the past two years, sushi has become cool Parisians' (read under-forty-year-old Parisians'—for most Parisians under forty years old are absolutely convinced of the fact that they are cool) food of choice. If a Parisian eats out for lunch with his colleagues every day, it is simply impossible not to go for sushi at least once a week. Impossible.

Sushi restaurants have flourished everywhere in Paris. They are usually owned and operated by Chinese people. It is amusing to notice that just like the other two dimensions of cool, sushi in Paris has mostly been made popular by Americans and is mostly made by Chinese people.

As the Parisian first starts eating sushi, he feels as though he is penetrating the secret and precious world of Japanese gastronomy, New York–style. The thrill of differentiating culinary exploration. He then realizes that sushi seems to be low in fat and rather cheap. So he starts consuming it more regularly—gains confidence. When the Parisian gains confidence, gentle respect and cryptic devotion turn into absurd self-importance and outrageous rudeness.

In most sushi restaurants in Paris, menus are quite comfortably repetitive and kindly made intelligible with pictures. Parisian men tend to opt for the sushi *brochettes* menu. Parisian women, in a noble attempt to minimize the caloric impact of their meal, usually favor sashimi. When the Parisian takes someone from *province* to a sushi restaurant, he will usually order for him and show him how to use chopsticks. The Parisian is well-traveled and always considerate.

On top of the myriad of Chinese-owned sushi places, Paris has become very big on sushi delivery. Restaurants that deliver are more into marketing and are not operated by Chinese people. Every other Parisian under forty years old orders sushi on Sunday nights.

Sooner or later, sushi eaters will claim to love Japanese food. *La cuisine japonaise, tu vois, c'est hyper fin, moi j'aime beaucoup.* ("Japanese cuisine is really refined: I love it.") Loving Japanese food implies nothing but enjoying sushi. The climax of this culinary escalation is the discovery of Rue Sainte-Anne. La Rue Sainte-Anne is Paris's little Tokyo: one Japanese restaurant after the other. On his first visit to a Japanese restaurant on Rue Sainte-Anne, the Parisian will enjoy the pioneering excitement of finally entering the world of "real" Japanese food, with "real" Japanese people cooking and waiting tables. On Rue Sainte-Anne, he will start dismissing sushi (ignorant food) and venture like the true explorer he has always been into sobas, udons, okonomiyakis. . . . He will then start taking friends to Rue Sainte-Anne—or more precisely taking them to *un p'tit resto japonais que j'adore, tu vas voir* (conveniently, that one restaurant is usually the only one he's been to). Taking friends there, the Parisian will systematically warn them with the hint of condescension that is the real cement of a true

Parisian friendship: *Attention par contre: c'est du vrai japonais, y a pas de sushi, hein.* ("Watch out though, this is real Japanese, no sushi there.")

Being beyond yet not over one of the attributes of cool is a very Parisian response to the dictatorship of cool: I'm still cool, but I'm also more than cool.

If you do the math that makes the Parisian super cool.

USEFUL TIP: Unless you love lines, don't try Rue Sainte-Anne on a Saturday night.

SOUND LIKE A PARISIAN: *Oh, hier soir, j'suis resté à la maison, tranquillou, commandé des sushis, rien de spécial.* ("Last night I had a quiet night at home, I ordered in sushi, nothing special.")

Saying They Like Classical Music

Though to most Parisians "Quatre Saisons" rings a pizza bell, Rameau has to do with church, and Rossini is a way to prepare meat, Parisians are all big-time into classical music. Classical music is one of the things Parisians are unable not to claim they like. To the question *T'écoutes quoi comme musique?*, most Parisians will respond saying: *Oh, un peu de tout: des conneries à la radio, un peu de chanson française, Brel, Brassens et puis un peu de classique.* ("A little bit of everything: pop songs, French songs, Brel, Brassens, and a bit of classical music.")

The Parisian at this point never gets more specific. He never shares his love for Bach or Liszt. He never mentions a symphony he never gets tired of. His public effusions for classical music—when elaborated on—are always justified by deep sentences like *ça me détend* or *ça me fait du bien.* Parisians never run short of grandiose homages.

Parisians will never challenge one another when it comes to classical music for they all share the same exact policy about it. This absence of escalation is rather un-Parisian and truly unconscious. Parisians' appreciation of classical music has been declared and repeated so many times that each Parisian ends up convincing himself that he does indeed like classical music. The fact that he never actually listens to classical music is no reasonable objection to this conviction.

ACADEMIE NATIONALE DE MUSIQUE
1770 BEETHOVEN 1827
1756 MOZART 1791

Each Parisian vividly recalls the three minutes last year on a drive to somewhere when he flipped through radio channels and stopped on classical music. After three minutes, he got bored and moved on. But those three minutes were times of vast satisfaction (to come).

The more educated the Parisian, the more his cultural references are unconsciously inflated. Saying he likes classical music is just one of the elements of the discreetly shiny cultural outfit the Parisian likes to wear socially: along the same lines, educated Parisians will enjoin their friends and acquaintances to *relire* such and such author, they will claim to love such and such writer while most likely only read one of his books, or they will pretend to have a deep knowledge of the Jewish culture for they had a Jewish friend in high school. All very much in good faith. Culture is vastly a masquerade in Paris.

Always a nonchalant one: when he runs across some classical music, it is impossible for the Parisian man not to whistle along.

In Paris more than anywhere else, silence can really be golden.

USEFUL TIP: Beautiful classical concerts are held inside the splendid Sainte-Chapelle. Look them up!

SOUND LIKE A PARISIAN: *Ouais, mais en même temps, tu vois, Hitler il adorait Wagner.* ("Sure, but at the same time, you know, Hitler loved listening to Wagner.")

Le Café Gourmand

Some questions define countries. *Fromage ou dessert?* once defined France. But France has changed, making this beautiful question obsolete, and the choice at the end of a meal even easier. For that question has shrunk to a monolithical interrogation: *Dessert?*

Modernity certainly comes at a price.

While dessert is worthy of a question, coffee never is. A meal without coffee in Paris is a bit like a day without alcohol in England. Something rare and peculiar. If there's a meal, there will be coffee to wrap it up.

Over the past few decades in Paris, dessert has supplanted cheese, then slowly dessert was supplanted by coffee. Ends of meals are that competitive in Paris. Recently, Parisians started blaming dessert for many of their own problems: dessert has become too pricey, too fattening, too time-consuming. Poor dessert. Meanwhile, coffee was bragging. Self-satisfied. Frequently accompanied with *un p'tit chocolat*—taunting dessert. Arrogant little thing.

Le café gourmand is a just attempt to reconcile coffee with dessert. On one plate: an espresso and an assortment of miniature desserts just seem to celebrate the glory of bitterness and sweetness brought together. Colorful and peaceful joy.

The assortment of desserts that comes with *le café gourmand* usually includes *un mini moelleux au chocolat, une mini crème brûlée, un mini clafoutis,* and *une petite boule de glace.* Mini and sweet is something that satisfies the Parisian. Mini sweet is mini sin.

The trick of *le café gourmand* is that, though it is minimum sin, it is maximum indulgence. You have it all. Coffee *and* dessert. And multiple desserts to top it off. Restaurateurs with *le café gourmand* become the Parisian's partners in crime: flattering his social sense of guilt, while stroking discreetly his shameful *gourmandise.*

Not sure you want to come across as though you still have room for dessert? *Le café gourmand* in its plentiful discretion is here for you.

It is worthy to know, though, that while ordering it for lunch is fully acceptable, ordering it for dinner is much more suspicious: what at lunchtime is viewed by fellow eaters as a charming expression of a sense of soft indulgence becomes in the evening a form of inability to fully enjoy. By some Parisian miracle, time of day started defining whether *le café gourmand* had a centripetal or centrifugal influence on the self.

In the end, the surge of *cafés gourmands* in Parisian *bistrots* and restaurants teaches us about the evolution of the status of *la gourmandise* in Paris: vice in the daytime, virtue at night.

Thank God for long and dark Parisian winters. . . .

USEFUL TIP: Screw people who make you feel bad for eating dessert.

SOUND LIKE A PARISIAN: *Oh ouais, tiens, un café gourmand, pourquoi pas, tiens! Alors, combien de cafés gourmands?* ("Oh sure, *café gourmand,* why not? Okay, guys, so how many?")

L'Ile Saint-Louis

When it comes to real estate, Parisians tend to settle for good enough. Thankfully enough. For if all Parisians lived where they really wanted to, l'Ile Saint-Louis would most likely drown.

L'Ile Saint-Louis has it all. It is central but isolated, beautiful but discreet, vibrant but quiet. L'Ile Saint-Louis is the essence of Paris. Its nest. Its most charming smile. No Parisian fails to notice that. Parisians are all irremediably in love with that island. Indefectible love—the type of love you know will never leave you. A love that ends up defining you.

Crossing that island feels good. Serene elegance is soothing. Beyond beautiful, it simply feels like home. You cross the island reassured. Reassured in beauty. This place seems untouched by the vicissitudes of urban life. This island does float.

Parisians make l'Ile Saint-Louis a destination for simple and timeless pleasures. A bike ride with the children, a kiss with a stranger, a gentle stroll with a spouse. Throughout a Parisian life, l'Ile Saint-Louis becomes, year after year, the theater of times to remember. As if of all bike rides, of all kisses, and of all strolls, the one on l'Ile Saint-Louis was more precious. L'Ile Saint-Louis embellishes moments. It gives every instant more depth and more flavor. L'Ile Saint-Louis makes life worth remembering.

Yet, l'Ile Saint-Louis is not a frequent destination for Parisians. L'Ile Saint-Louis pervades the Parisian's soul. Its beauty can be a cumbersome companion. There is little time for this. Dispossession of self is not a Parisian specialty, so the Parisian chooses carefully its Ile Saint-Louis moments. Mostly, let's face it, for romantic masterplans or Berthillon expeditions. But sometimes, the stroll will have no point but itself. *La promenade* will in that case always be bittersweet. Time passing by. Parisians like it bittersweet.

L'Ile Saint-Louis is like a bottle thrown in Paris's ocean. A *promenade* there is a way to try to get to the message inside. The message is hard to read. But some words just seem to be there, every time. Telling us something.

Something about an island, and about a continent.

USEFUL TIP: Go late at night.

SOUND LIKE A PARISIAN: *Non, vraiment, si j'avais le choix, mon rêve, ca serait d'avoir un appart' sur l'Ile Saint-Louis.* ("No really, if I had the choice, my dream would be to have an apartment on l'Ile Saint-Louis.")

Considering Americans Stupid

Parisians have a bit of a different physiology. Things like a certain inability to smile are quite well-known expressions of this phenomenon. Some are much lesser known: an interesting experience when chatting with a Parisian is to place the words *les Américains* in a sentence. These two words put together—in any imaginable sentence—immediately trigger a chemical reaction in the Parisian's brain. When hearing the phrase *les Américains,* the Parisian will implacably lose track of his previous ideas to be taken over by one overpowering thought. That is: *Oui, mais les Américains, ils sont cons.*

There is no exception to that rule. Americans are all stupid. End of story. The fact that the United States is the most successful and probably the most creative country in the world is not an argument. Nor is the fact that all Parisians deliberately wear American clothes, watch American movies, listen to American music, use American words, or fantasize about American celebrities. Americans are fat, stupid, and ugly. Period.

Parisians who have traveled to the United States might have a more moderate opinion: they will view Americans as *superficiels.* Parisians of all classes see every interaction entailing a person from the United States as irremediably fake and empty. Traveling surely makes Parisians more in touch with foreign cultures.

The immediate friendliness most Americans display at once sends Parisians insane. *Mais pourquoi ils sourient? Ils sont cons ou quoi?!* ("But why are they smiling, are they idiots or what?") Friendliness, enthusiasm, and optimism are very American qualities. In Paris, these characteristics are marks of gentle intellectual decay. You do the math. In the Parisian's mind, Americans are incapable of refinement. Capital Parisian sin. Whether their vision is based on reality or not has no relevance: of course it is.

Parisians know for a fact that Americans' exclusive interests are money, sports, war, and religion. Americans have no other points of interest in life. No other aspirations. That is good enough a reason for Parisians to concentrate most of their scorn for the opulence of Western life on America. It's all America's fault. It is true after all that Parisians by no means partake in this Western lifestyle.

When bringing to the table that not everyone in a country like America can possibly be stupid, the Parisian usually pulls out the culture card. *OK, peut-être, mais ils sont complètement incultes, c'est grave quand même.* ("OK, maybe, but they are completely ignorant, it's unbelievable.") People saying this fall into two categories: on the one hand, people whose favorite after-work occupations consist of watching *CSI*, *Grey's Anatomy*, or *Sex and the City*; on the other, people who worship Woody Allen and Philip Roth. Parisians are avid consumers of American culture and at the same time fiercely convinced that such a thing does not exist. For as Parisians put it, *Woody Allen, il est pas Américain, il est New-Yorkais.*

It would be impolite at that point to bring to the Parisian's attention that he starts to sound like the stupid American he despises so much. Plus, despite his obvious in-depth knowledge of America, chances are he might not get the joke. . . .

USEFUL TIP: Rest assured, most people interacting with tourists know better. They appreciate Americans' friendliness and taste for good service (read tips). So you're in good shape. For the optimal Paris experience, leave your New Balance shoes at home.

SOUND LIKE A PARISIAN: "Oh my God, it's amazing! Ha ha ha."

100%
PARISIEN
APPROUVÉ

Cherry Tomatoes

Louis Armstrong says tomato. No matter what, so does Ella Fitzgerald. Parisians, on the other hand, prefer to say cherry tomato.

Parisians are that cool.

Meet the thrilling cherry tomato. All the qualities of a tomato, minus the defects. When asked "Why cherry tomatoes?" all Parisians would agree that *J'sais pas. J'aime bien et puis ça change.* ("I don't know. I like them, plus they're just different.") Say no more, impetuous Parisian—change is your passion, we all know that. We understand. *Adieu tomate. Bonjour tomate cerise.*

Cherry tomatoes are everywhere in Paris. In restaurants, a quarter of a cherry tomato does wonders to decorate a plate. At a supermarket, neglectfully placing *une boîte de tomates cerises* in your cart shows everyone around that you can afford that extra euro. At home, cherry tomatoes have the good taste of needing no slicing. Minimal effort, maximum effect. There is now no inviting friends over for a casual dinner without serving cherry tomatoes as an addition to your aperitif. *C'est tout simple mais c'est sympa, c'est frais.* ("Simple and fresh.")

This evolution has had tragic consequences on the Paris food scene. First collateral victim: *la salade de tomates.* Cherry tomatoes now make presenting a plate with actual tomatoes in it cheap and passé. RIP *salade de tomates.* Thankfully, the

Parisian leaves Paris at times. When his peregrinations take him *en province*, he may notice that old-school *tomates* still exist there. Making him resolute to give tomatoes a second chance. Organic tomatoes that time.

Needless to say these resolutions won't last too long in front of the cherry tomato shelf. Seductive little things . . .

USEFUL TIP: The more you slice your cherry tomato, the more civilized you will appear.

SOUND LIKE A PARISIAN: *J'ai invité Nico et Elisa pour l'apéro. Tu peux passer chez Monop s'te plait?! Tu prends une bouteille de rosé, un peu de saucisson, et des tomates cerises. Moi, je me grouille, je passe à la boulangerie avant que ça ferme!* ("I invited Nico and Elisa over for appetizers. Can you stop at the store please? Get a bottle of rosé, some charcuterie, and cherry tomatoes. I'll hurry up and swing by the bakery before it closes!")

The Word *Putain*

The noun *putain* refers to a prostitute. The interjection *putain* refers to no one. In its most common usage, it simply vividly expresses utterly Parisian feelings like discontentment, anger, and frustration—stuck in a traffic jam: *Putain, mais c'est pas possible*; talking about her boss: *Il est complètement con, putain* . . . In those instances, the word works as a very Parisian capital letter or full stop. It is by far the most common usage of the word.

But the reach of the word goes beyond this initial scope. *Putain* in Paris also defines surprise—witnessing a car accident: *Oh putain*; watching the clock: *Putain, il est déjà deux heures?* It can also be a firm injunction to stop joking around: *Putain, t'es serieux?*, *Attends putain, deux secondes.* In the same realm, used on its own, *putain* in a conversation can express sympathy and interest when a sad subject is being talked about.

Parisian 1: *Et c'est là que son mari l'a quittée.* ("And that's when her husband left her.")
Parisian 2: *Putain.*

Awkwardly enough, it can also express admiration or encouragement—talking about a really good movie: *Putain, c'était hyper bien*; discovering a friend's new apartment; *Putainnn*; hearing that someone they knew took a trip around the world: *Putain?*; watching a game on TV: *Allez putain!*

When followed by *de, putain* is used to emphasize: *Il a une putain de voiture.* ("He's got a *putain* of a car.") *C'est un putain de restaurant.* ("It's a *putain* of a restaurant.") This last usage is the only one that will be considered rude. Simply because it is the only instance where Parisians will actually hear themselves using the word.

In the end, the word *putain* in Paris is used to express surprise, anger, encouragement, frustation, emphasis, or admiration. In the case of Parisians, extensive use of the word *putain,* in its most frequent sense, shows the social need for anger, roughness, and frustration. These are social necessities in Paris. If you are not angry about most events of life, and not ready to swear about it or even notice when you do, you clearly are not a Parisian. *Putain* is just another tool to blend in. Running around when everybody walks with crutches would be straight-up rude. The choice is simple for people who live in Paris: sprinkle every one of your sentences with a *putain* or go find a city of your own.

While it certainly is helpful, extensive use of crutches has one disadvantage: it creates atrophies and muscular unbalances. The outcome of using *putain* extensively in Paris is a form of mental laziness. Making up emptiness with easy negativity: absence concealed behind a word.

USEFUL TIP: If you don't know what to say, just say *putain.*

SOUND LIKE A PARISIAN: *Non mais putain . . . c'est pas possible bordel!* ("*Putain,* this can't be freaking true!")

Belgians

Parisians are all high-flying anthropologists. They know about other people and other countries. Expertly enough, they manage to synthesize their in-depth knowledge about the people of any given country down to one adjective. This adjective cannot be challenged. Thus proving that it is accurate.

As an example, Americans are stupid, Portuguese are hairy, Vietnamese are Chinese, and Belgians are *sympa. . . . Ils sont sympas les Belges!* To cheer a Parisian up, there is nothing like mentioning the word *Belge.* Immediately, a joyful and smily heap of thoughts will invade the Parisian's mind.

The Parisian will be transported to a world of accents, *moules frites,* and people laughing. At this point, the Parisian will most likely come up with a silly sentence delivered with a poor Belgian accent. He will most likely end that sentence with assumed Belcisim *une fois. Mah tu n'es pas un peu con, une fois . . .* ("Aren't you a little stupid, *une fois . . .*") Very rarely in his life will a Parisian be as happy as right after he comes up with such a sentence. Genuine Parisian bliss.

While Belgian jokes are a French humor classic, Parisians never crack one. Too risky for their image. But they love *les Belges* even more as they can consider them through that comforting buffer of superiority that decades of Belgian jokes have established precisely at the border between France and

Belgium. This buffer of superiority is emphasized by the Belgians' drinking habits: *Tu veux une bière, une fois?!* ("You want a beer, *une fois?!*") Parisians truly look down on anyone who drinks. Interestingly, this perception is slightly amended for *les Belges.* Parisians find their drinking habits if not cute at least typical—and ultimately quite entertaining. The fact that a Belgian could be sad or not joyful is not something the Parisian is ready to cope with. Belgians are joyful, generally drunk, and speak with a funny accent.

Period.

Parisians love spending time with Belgians. But these moments can only be occasional. The Parisian who spends time with Belgians runs the risk of gaining some form of lightheartedness. Parisians know better than hedging such a risk. Social threat.

Two elements tarnish what otherwise would be a true perfect relationship for the Parisian. One, that half of the Belgians are Dutch (for *Les Hollandais, ils sont chiants*). Two, this habit the other half of Belgians have to use *savoir* (to know) for *pouvoir* (can/to be able). As in, *Tu saurais me passer le sel, s'il te plaît.* ("You know to pass me the salt, please.") Other Belgian phrases amuse Parisians. This one makes them cringe. All the more so because the Belgian won't change this habit—even when asked to do so by a Parisian. Disrepectful Belgians after all? The Parisian prefers to see them as children—*de grands enfants* (disrespectful being something the Parisian can never be).

On top of the favorite topics talked about with a Belgian ranks Belgian politics. The Parisian knows nothing about Belgian politics except for the fact that the country is about to burst. The Parisian knows that for sure. And that's all the Belgian politics he wants to talk about. The only relevant question in Belgian politics to the Parisian is: when is Belgium becoming part of France? At this point, *le Belge* usually says something about Brittany or Corsica. Then the Parisian gets offended. And talks about sex scandals in Belgium or Johnny Hallyday.

In no time at all, a Parisian with the best intentions in the world turned a cloudless relationship into an embarassing fight scene. Had the Parisian stuck to his initial "Entertain me, Belgian man" ways, things would have been just fine.

Really, good intentions and Parisians don't seem to work well together. *Une fois.*

USEFUL TIP: Read the comic *Le Chat* by the kind and talented Belgian Philippe Geluck—funny stuff.

SOUND LIKE A PARISIAN: *On a rencontré des Belges en vacances, hyper sympa. . . . Tu vois, elle, bon humour, sympa, lui, gros déconneur, très sympa aussi. Par contre, qu'est-ce qu'ils picolent!* ("We met some Belgians on holiday, really great people. . . . You know she was funny and nice, and he was a joker and nice as well. But, man, do they drink!")

Moderation

If qualities were diseases, moderation would be the Parisian plague.

In Paris, no London style, no Vegas drunks, and no Rio bodies.

Parisians prefer to the thrill of the full-on ride the comfort of the gray cocoon.

Excess is vulgar. So they will not indulge. They will not even give it a try. Admittedly, there is no need to give things a try when you know about them already.

Parisians never go all the way. Parisians never order that second bottle of wine. How crass. They seem to find more contentment in witnessing things than in living them. They somewhat cherish that distance. Distance is a Parisian's best friend. A buffer between him and life. A seat belt between him and his own life. Excess is not safe. Parisians like it safe.

In Paris, the plague has gone rampant. Moderation that once was a vague companion has become the inspiration of every decision. From the smallest one to the most decisive. A whole life governed by fear. A whole life of resolute blending in. A life dedicated to not making waves.

One may think that moderation is a form of preservation of an existing happiness. That is not true in Paris—simply because no Parisian would ever present himself (let alone think of himself) as happy. The Parisian just preserves whatever it is he has. Even if he's far from satisfied with it. Parisians never put themselves out there. They never aim high. Never go for the big prize. They are careful. Dreadfully careful. Excess implies forgetting about oneself for a second. There is in excess a true form of generosity. A willingness to let go and connect with others. There laid the foundations of the late joie de vivre.

Parisians even lost sight that a whole world exists between moderation and excess. This world brings unknown and newness to the table. The Parisian is very happy not to have to deal with these. He knows very well that outside moderation only exist things like outrage and emptiness. The Parisian is too wise. Deal with it.

When it comes to fun, true fun in Paris is necessarily associated with excess. And therefore carefully dodged. True fun is ultimately outrageous and empty. There is no point in having real fun. Soft fun is good enough. At least it's safe.

The same pathological approach to reality has contaminated all fields of Parisian society. From politics to arts, from conversations to looks: moderation has taken over minds, souls, and closets.

Paris has become a tepid city full of tepid people.

USEFUL TIP: Resist.

SOUND LIKE A PARISIAN: *Bon allez, je vais rentrer, je suis crevé en ce moment. C'était cool, on devrait se refaire ça un de ces jours.* ("OK, I'm gonna go home now, I'm exhausted. It was nice though, we should get together again soon.")

Stars

In Paris, horizons and perspectives were all defined by man. Infinity stops right at the other end of the street. Looking up uncovers a narrow stripe of gray. Looking down as well. For Parisians, looking inside is therefore the only possibility to fathom infinity.

One of the greatest pleasures *la province* treats the Parisian to is an immediate sense of the grandiosity of nature. Repressed in his city high, he lives most days with comfort and ease in nothing but concrete. Leaving the city opens new doors. It offers a new form of enchantment. The enchantment of awe. Very few things leave the Parisian belittled, somewhere between admiration and fear.

Stars do.

There are few things Parisians like as much as discovering a night sky sprinkled with stars. Coming out of a house after a nice dinner, coming out of a car after a long drive, the Parisian is caught off guard by the disdainful beauty of the night. He finds himself charmed and thrilled by this view that exceeds him. Finally something does.

Stars don't like competition. They prefer not to show in the City of Light. Seeing them is therefore a rare instance for Parisians. The emotion the Parisian feels under the stars is similar to the one he feels when faced with a raging ocean or quiet

mountain range. An emotion away from home, a break from the petty. An invitation to somewhere intimate.

Stars comfort the Parisian in the idea that there is more to life than the mediocrity and ugliness he finds himself surrounded with. He feels close to that superior unknown.

So he will smile.

USEFUL TIP: Know that Milky Way to a French person will forever be the name of a chocolate bar.

SOUND LIKE A PARISIAN: *Oh, t'as vu les étoiles!* ("Oh, look at the stars!")

Le Marché

Parisians love *le marché* (the market).

Truth be told, most Parisians buy their groceries from supermarkets. Only two types of Parisians go to *le marché* to fill up their carts with groceries: those are elderly Parisians and housewives.

Elderly Parisian women take advantage of years of accumulated *marché* wisdom—combined, it is true, with the tortuous

roads of sleep in old age—to take over the *marché* at the earliest hours of the day. Between 7:00 and 9:00 a.m., *le marché* is a charming place, full of elderly ladies, eager to bring home nothing but the best groceries.

As the morning unfolds, the scene changes, elderly women leave *le marché*. Parisian housewives get in with their strollers or their carts. Parisian housewives need wheels. That's how they roll.

For all other Parisians, on weekdays *le marché* is just a reassuring encounter, a taste of *province* on their way to work. But everything changes on the weekend. Some Parisians are lucky enough to have a *marché* near them on Saturday or Sunday mornings. These *marchés* offer simple visions of a Parisian wonderland. Discreet perfection. Parisians playfully enjoy the charms of their local *marché*. With its characteristic colors, smells, and sounds, everything at *le marché* evokes a form of timeless simplicity. *Le marché du weekend* is a treat. Parisians feel as though they are doing themselves some good. Connecting again with simple pleasures, with simple people. *Le marché du weekend* is about letting go—between leeks and potatoes.

Among the weekend *marché*-goers, some Parisians are just too cool to go to *le marché* for strict grocery shopping purposes. How common. They go to *le marché* for the vibe. Sure, they shop a little, but they're primarily there for the quaint atmosphere. No matter how much they like *le marché*, it is important for these people to show that this is not what they do. The cool Parisian goes to *le marché* in an eminently neglected outfit. That gives him the impression of being a New Yorker. Heavens. Sunglasses are almost an imperative accessory for cool Parisians at *le marché*: in that they testify of the greatness of the previous night, they show that *le Parisien* does *le marché* a favor by simply being there. He's a tourist—visiting for a minute a normal person's life.

Whether he's in for the carrots or the vibe, the Parisian likes his *marché.* He finds nothing but comfort in this well-orchestrated scenography. Fleeting yet familiar moments. Rich of people and fruits, of smiles and colors. *Le marché* is the ultimate Parisian halt. A halt in motion and in noises. A halt that refuses to be one. At *le marché,* Parisians consider time with modesty, walking, playing, and sniffing: taking for a few minutes the chance of tastier moments.

USEFUL TIP: The best fruits and vegetables will be found at the beginning of *le marché*; the best prices at the end of it.

SOUND LIKE A PARISIAN: *Ce weekend, c'était top: samedi matin, on a fait le marché avec Baptiste, après on a cuisiné toute l'après-midi . . . tu sais, on avait nos amis sud-africains qui venaient dîner à la maison.* ("This weekend was really great: Saturday morning I went to the market with Baptiste, then we cooked all afternoon . . . you know, we had our South African friends over for dinner.")

Crossing the Street in a Bold Way

Traffic on the streets of Paris may seem chaotic and disorganized. Parisians seem to roar in a chaos of metal and gray. These are misconceptions. Traffic in Paris is actually harmonious, and Parisians feel nothing but comfort in it. Road rules in Paris are simply vastly unwritten rules.

Some of these unwritten rules regulate normal driving techniques, others define an acceptable insult level, and others set a social frame around the interactions between drivers and pedestrians.

In Paris, the sidewalk belongs (mostly) to pedestrians and the road (mostly) to automobiles.

Mopeds, bicycles, and all other rolling objects tend to choose whichever option seems like the most convenient for them given the state of traffic. Alternating is OK—but drivers of two-wheelers should in that case be prepared to face older pedestrians' grumblings.

When it comes to cars and pedestrians, all Parisians know that a car won't stop for a pedestrian. Especially at a pedestrian crossing. A car that actually stops at a pedestrian crossing will be honked at and its driver immediately suspected of provinciality. Knowing that they don't belong at pedestrian crossings, Parisians cross the street mostly randomly. So it's only logical that Parisians cross the street whenever they feel like it or whenever there is a break in traffic.

The only Parisians crossing at pedestrian crossings are old folks. The rest of the crowd standing there is made up of *banlieusards*, *provinciaux*, and tourists. This comforts the Parisian car driver in the conviction that stopping to yield to pedestrians is a bizarre idea.

Since they cross the street in undue places, Parisian pedestrians have to compete with cars for road domination. Parisians are well exercised urban beings.

They have no fear and they demonstrate it. By engaging the road with brutal authority. Tourists mistake authority for insanity. Foolish!

But authority, deprived of a sense of politeness, is disturbing to most Parisians. It lacks beauty. To reenchant road crossing, Parisians unconsciously initiate an elegant dance. A dance made up of confidence in your fellow Parisian. "I dominate you, but I trust you." Refinement in this dance is to cross the street while keeping your walking pace absolutely unchanged from one side of the road to the other. As in an urban bullfight, the closer you cross to the running car and the faster the car is going, the more thrilling, the more beautiful the move. Parisians caress cars.

In this urban sensuality, the Parisian feels the thrill of full mastery of the city and its codes. He is at home. Even in the simplest act of crossing the street, the Parisian—half dancer, half bullfighter—stays true to his blurry but confident identity. Always secretly inviting others to watch, learn, and admire.

USEFUL TIP: In order to look Parisian, never stand at a red light waiting for it to turn green. There has to be a better way.

SOUND LIKE A PARISIAN: *Attends, viens, on traverse.* ("Hold on, come on, let's cross.")

La San Pé

Parisians have always indulged. Today is no different. Parisians still indulge.

Mostly in fizzy water.

When ordering fizzy water, Parisians feel the thrill of excitement running down their spine. The taste of rebellion. The frivolous flavors of a bubbly world. Parisians are fearless. And conquering such mountains of sparkling unknown brings a genuine satisfaction to their table. A satisfaction only real adventurers get to experience.

The world of sparkling waters in Paris is a fast-changing one. The eighties were pioneering years with Perrier. The nineties saw the triumph of Badoit. But all these were mere preparations for the new millennium's crowning. That of the queen of all fizzy waters: la San Pé.

Parisians deep inside are tender. And loving. Precisely for that reason, they will not name their favorite water San Pellegrino. In Paris, San Pellegrino has become San Pé. A Parisian's liquid best friend. At a restaurant, Parisian males are especially fond of sharp and killer orders like *"Deux onglets saignants et une San Pé."* Pure Parisian testosterone.

Parisians can't resist the attraction of San Pé's precise and gentle bubble. Vaguely retro, vaguely new, and vaguely healthy, San Pé fills the Parisian's need for soft and stroking authenticity. But San Pé does more than quench the Parisian's thirst, tickle his tongue, and enchant his environment. It also helps the Parisian regain at a decent price some social differentiation credits.

San Pé is indeed the gift that keeps giving. And it treats two of his attributes the Parisian likes to take care of the most: his palate and his ego. His palate is flattered by San Pé's gentle and precise bubble. His ego by the double pleasure of ordering it, and paying for it. Few Parisians have friends that do them as much good as San Pé does.

By drinking San Pé, the Parisian does not drink tap. He is therefore perceived by his fellow Parisians as superior. Three reasons for that: he has taste, money, and a sense of indulgence. These are characteristics most Parisians wish they could boast.

Thus making anyone who does not order San Pé at a business lunch somewhat of a loser.

Santé!

USEFUL TIP: San Pellegrino is owned by Nestlé. Remember this to counter frequent attacks that San Pé is originally Italian.

SOUND LIKE A PARISIAN: *Un crudités-poulet et une San Pé.* ("Chicken salad sandwich and a San Pé.")

Southern Accents

Parisians see the south of France as one. It is *le sud.*

While *Toulousains, Niçois,* or *Montpellierains* come from three very distinct regions of France, they are viewed in Paris as *du sud.* As such, they all have *l'accent du sud.*

All Parisians love *l'accent du sud.* There is no exception to that rule.

L'accent du sud twists the French language with a softer, more *chantant* touch. While Parisians mock the Alsatian, Swiss, or Northern accents, they cannot get enough of *l'accent du sud.* Anyone speaking with *l'accent du sud* will immediately score high points on the friendliness scale. As Parisians wisely put it: *Les gens du sud sont hyper sympa.* ("Southern folks are really friendly.")

Hearing *l'accent du sud* takes the Parisian straight on holiday. The sun shines in his heart. He is thankful for that. So he might take it as far as trying to be friendly with the people from the south of France. Friendly back somehow! Thus suddenly acting very awkward. Most *sudistes* at this point get overwhelmed with discomfort and prefer to leave it there. It is hard for Parisians to befriend someone with *l'accent du sud.* Really.

Soon enough, *l'accent du sud* becomes a cultural barrier the Parisian can't seem to break down. While building up cultural barriers is usually every Parisian's prime craft and favorite pastime, this one cultural barrier affects him deeply. Realizing that a person with *l'accent du sud* will always come across as nicer and more fun than him makes the Parisian secretly frustrated.

So he will retaliate.

By making fun of people with *l'accent du sud.* Parisians love to imitate *l'accent du sud* to portray stupid people. If a Parisian recounts a story to his friends of getting pulled over by a police officer, every word spoken by the policeman will be transcripted with *l'accent du sud.*

This strategy of assimilating nice people to stupid people exquisitely satisfies the Parisian. And allows him to dominate his frustration. Ultimately, *l'accent du sud* is more than an ear-pleasing enchantment to the Parisian; it is an ego-boosting delight.

USEFUL TIP: When Parisians put a "g" at the end of a word when they speak (*loing, cong, putaing*), it means they are trying to imitate *l'accent du sud.*

SOUND LIKE A PARISIAN: *Oh, t'as l'accent du sud . . . c'est génial.* ("Oh, you have *l'accent du Sud,* that's really great.")

Considering Artists as Slackers

Parisians all work hard. They have little tolerance for people who do not work hard.

Parisians know that one category of people never works: artists. Artists are the biggest slackers. Parisians hardly have any respect for them. The only respectable artists are the dead ones. All other artists—in the Parisian's mind—are just crooks.

Parisians assimilate artists to *intermittents. Intermittent du spectacle* is an advantageous treatment the French government came up with to offer *protection sociale* to artists. This system is an endless financial well, paid for by nonartists. Knowing that their hard work is subsidizing artists' absence of work drives most Parisians crazy. Hence triggering a brutal rejection of artists. The concept of art in the Parisian's mind has to do with posterity. It has to do with greatness.

Most Parisians consider artists to be socially useless. If objected to that some artists drive substantial revenues for their industries—besides the cultural and aesthetic satisfaction their work generates—the Parisian will quickly respond that these people are not artists. They are *des vendus qui font de la merde* ("sellouts who make shit"). Then the word "marketing" usually comes in the following sentence. Marketing is a very degrading thing to be involved with in Paris. Placing "artist" and "marketing" in the same sentence is the biggest offense a Parisian could come up with.

The Parisian likes to see artists struggle. The artist is to be broke. Broke means talented and real for the Parisian.

On the other hand, all successful artists are primarily marketing people. The Parisian knows that.

The same reasoning applies to the style of artists. Real artists need to have greasy hair and act tormented. An artist who looks good is a crook.

In many countries, students go to college to study the trade and craft of art for several years. France hardly offers such programs. People who make a living from arts are suspicious in the Parisians' degree-structured brains. Artists are like fortune-tellers or life coaches: suspicious. All the more suspicious as the Parisian knows for a fact that no skills are required to be an artist. Writing? Painting? Singing? Acting? Any Parisian could do at least two of these things just as well as any so-called professional.

It's true that the Parisian is talented. Making him somewhat of an artist. Just a potential one.

USEFUL TIP: The word *artistique* does not work as a compliment in Paris.

SOUND LIKE A PARISIAN: *Ambiance artiste, un peu dégueu, je fume des joints . . . tu vois le genre quoi!* ("The vibe was sort of artistic, kinda dirty, pot-smoking type . . . you know what I mean!")

P'tits Weekends

Parisians all get sick of Paris after a while.

So they regularly choose to leave the city for a few days.

Those expeditions are called *p'tits weekends.*

Le weekend is Saturday and Sunday. And it takes place in Paris.

Le p'tit weekend is those two days for sure, plus potentially one or two before or after. And it takes place somewhere outside Paris.

The destination and frequency of the *p'tits weekends* depend on the Parisian.

It is important to realize that in the Parisian's mind, *le p'tit weekend* is not a luxury or a treat. It is a necessity. A need he feels deep inside his body. A sound door to escape momentarily the oppression of the big, fast, and loud city: *J'en peux plus, faut que je parte m'aérer. Tu veux pas qu'on se fasse un p'tit weekend?* ("I've had enough, I need to leave the city to get some air. You want to go on a *p'tit weekend*?")

Le p'tit weekend can take place in the Parisian family house, in Normandy, in Brittany, in Burgundy, or in the south. But *le p'tit weekend*, being an utterly cool and stress-free concept, cannot happen with too much family around (anyone having a family knows that spending the weekend with them is neither cool nor stress-free): *Mes parents sont au Maroc. On peut se faire un p'tit weekend chez moi en Sologne si tu veux.* ("My parents

are in Morocco. We could have a *p'tit weekend* at my house in Sologne if you'd like.")

But usually, *le p'tit weekend* serves another purpose: that of allowing the Parisian to brag at work the following week. Bragging implies sunshine (*le sud*), or gentle *dépaysement.* Being very wise, the Parisian usually looks for *dépaysement* in another big European capital.

Needless to say there is an unwritten ranking of coolness in big European cities. Top-ranking cities are Barcelona, Berlin, and London. Maximum bragging.

For *un p'tit weekend en amoureux* (romantic declination of the *p'tit weekend*), high points go to Prague, Vienna, and Budapest. For *Parisiens,* Eastern European capitals are considered the utmost destinations for *un p'tit weekend entre potes* (let's-get-drunk-and-act-out-for-a-weekend—away-from-the-girlfriends sort of deal).

Eastern European capitals make *Parisiennes* worried.

Un p'tit weekend outside Europe or *au ski* is also an option, but sends the clear message that money is not a problem. The mention of such weekends will only be made in the appropriate circles. When asked how his *p'tit weekend* was, the Parisian has only two adjectives in mind: *super* and *excellent. P'tit weekends* are never anything but that.

In all cases, the Parisian is happy to share that *ça m'a trop fait du bien de partir un peu.* ("It felt so good to get away for a bit.") Since well-being and coolness are addictive, the Parisian prefers to experience them only by injections.

Two- or three-day ones are ideal.

USEFUL TIP: If you wish to see your Parisian friends in April, May, and June, let them know early. Major *p'tit weekend* season!

SOUND LIKE A PARISIAN: *Non, mais sérieux, Budapest, avec Easyjet, ca coûte vraiment que dalle. Tu devrais trop le faire.* ("Really, Budapest on Easyjet costs nothing. You should really go.")

Olive Oil

Parisians are beings of refinement and taste.

Bad luck for butter.

Butter is gross. And fattening. Parisians can't deal with butter.

Thankfully, Parisians over the past decade have found out about olive oil.

Discovering olive oil has been a treat for most Parisians, because it has allowed them to start despising butter. It always feels good to despise a new thing. Especially for a reason: it is obvious Parisian knowledge that olive oil is so much better than butter. Parisians do believe that olive oil is not fattening. There are no nuisances whatsoever associated with olive oil.

Switching from butter to olive oil is a natural thing for the Parisian. Olive oil corresponds to a vision of the world he is simply more receptive to. Agriculture as a business conducted by professionals in a rainy region is suspicious to the Parisian. Too much suffering, work, and weird smells involved. The Parisian much prefers a form of agriculture carried out under the sun of Provence by *un passionné*. So much better really. All in all, not only does olive oil do some good to the Parisian's body, but it also soothes his mind.

Only one other condiment comes with as much glow and sunny glamour as olive oil. That is balsamic vinegar. Anything made with *huile d'olive* or *vinaigre balsamique* can only be good. Of course.

On the other hand, anything made with butter or *crème* can only be heavy and fat. Other types of vinegars are for losers. If he really has to buy butter, the Parisian will not indulge in regular butter. He will opt for *beurre salé* or *demi-sel.* Why? *Parce que c'est dix fois meilleur.* Of course.

There is no point in reminding Parisians that all the dishes they fall for at a restaurant are made with significant amounts of butter and cream. Enchantment is rare enough a phenomenon in Paris to have any desire to blow its shiny bubble off.

Be it an extra-virgin bubble.

USEFUL TIP: Vinaigrette rocks.

SOUND LIKE A PARISIAN: *Tu vois, une petite salade, un filet d'huile d'olive, c'est tout simple, c'est hyper bon.* ("A small salad with a drizzle of olive oil is simple and tastes great.")

Le Monde

Parisians don't really trust the media.

They are media addicts. But they know better than to trust the media. There is one exception to that rule: *Le Monde. Le Monde* is a French newspaper. It is to the Parisian the one and only reliable source of information on earth.

No other country could ever achieve the level of independence and intellectual sharpness the French press offers consistently on a daily basis. In the Parisian's mind, news overseas can only be obtained through four channels: CNN, Al Jazeera, Fox News, and English tabloids. None of these are trustworthy. That is sadly all foreigners have access to. The Parisian feels a certain satisfaction from the fact that France is the only country in the world with actual newspapers.

The Parisian is too educated not to know that among French newspapers, very few are actually worth his time. *Libération, c'est hyper à gauche;* Le Figaro, *c'est hyper à droite; L'Equipe, ça va, j'suis pas un beauf non plus. Libération* is too leftist; *Le Figaro,* too rightist; *L'Equipe,* I'm not a *beauf.* The Parisian wants the press he reads to be freed from political beliefs, to be beyond them. Parisians like anything that is beyond.

Very few Parisians actually read *Le Monde.* Yet, all agree that *Le Monde, c'est un bon journal. Un journal sérieux,* too. Yes,

Parisians do have opinions about things they are not familiar with. Call that talent.

Parisians who actually read *Le Monde* are quickly put by other Parisians in the *intello* category. This category in some Parisian circles comes with a high level of desirability. Which makes some Parisians buy *Le Monde* on a regular basis, and just carry it around. In that case, the Parisian will always say with a sad look, *"C'est chiant, j'ai jamais le temps de le lire." Oui, c'est chiant.* The people who read *Le Monde* the least are the people who have a subscription to it. In that case, the plan is never to read the newspaper but to actually drop neglectfully in every other conversation a *J'suis abonné au Monde.*

Pure superiority.

USEFUL TIP: To be mistaken for a Parisian, buy *Le Monde*, fold it, and walk. Then sit at a café and make phone calls.

SOUND LIKE A PARISIAN: *Moi, de toute façon, je lis qu'Le Monde. Les autres journaux, honnêtement, j'peux pas.* ("In any event, I really only read *Le Monde*. I honestly can't read the other papers.")

Thinking That Not Wearing White Socks Makes You a Better Person

Parisians do believe that most human beings are respectable. Except for those wearing white socks.

Seeing someone wearing white socks provokes an immediate and brutal reaction inside the Parisian. He is suddenly taken over by disgust and scorn. The white socks wearer is immediately removed from the community of human beings.

As lenient as the Parisians would like to be, they simply cannot let some things slide.

High standards make the Parisian harsh at times. The sight of white socks makes Parisians sigh. They feel that such poor taste should not be allowed.

When it comes to colors of socks, Parisians stop being liberal. White socks worn with *chaussures de ville* are the worst of *fautes de goût*; they are a clear indicator of *appartenance sociale*.

Everyone wearing white socks is a *gros beauf*. Parisians want none of that around. Seeing a *gros beauf* on TV makes the Parisian laugh. But seeing one right near him, live in sock-offense mode, is an insult the Parisian cannot cope with. Some liberals assert that white socks worn with *des tennis* is OK. Truth is, it could only be OK if worn on a sports court. Anywhere else would be accumulating two *fautes de goût*: sneakers and white socks. Game over.

Wearing white socks ranks first in the Parisian pantheon of *mauvais goût vestimentaire.* Number two is for sure short-sleeved shirts.

A Nobel Prize winner wearing white socks will always remain to the Parisian a *"gros beauf* who's good at science or whatever it is he's good at, I don't care, he's just a *beauf putain how on earth is is possible to wear white socks like this, I can't believe it".* Sadly enough, in the world, most people put progress of science and humanity ahead of sock color in defining the quality of an individual. But Parisians know the type of socks these people are wearing.

Yes, for the Parisian, sometimes, indeed, things are a bit lonely in this world.

USEFUL TIP: When traveling to Paris, don't go there. Really, it won't serve your cause.

SOUND LIKE A PARISIAN: *Non, enfin, le mec, chaussettes blanches, manches courtes—la totale quoi, l'enfer!* ("Seriously, that guy was just a gigantic loser: white socks, short sleeves—he was full-on!")

Snow

Parisians are all grown-ups. They have no time to fool around. Life is too serious for that.

Most Parisians are very happy with their grown-upness—growing up in Paris was not all that fun, anyway. In the course of a lifetime, only one thing is susceptible to bring the Parisian back to a state comparable to that of a child. That is snow. Amusement parks don't do much for Parisians. Snow does.

Snow is a very rare thing in Paris. No living Parisian has woken up to snow more than twenty times in his life. It may snow in Paris every other year. Usually for twenty minutes. Parisians love snow. Snow in Paris is evanescent. Never sticks. In this evanescence lies the beauty and charm Parisians fall for.

The instant the first snowflake falls down, a Parisian (usually, the most idle one) will say, *"Oh, il neige."* Because snow is a hardly conceivable concept in Paris, the Parisian will systematically confirm the news: *"Regardez, il neige."*

Other Parisians in the room will *regarder*. Indeed, *il neige*. Usually, much cheesy talking ensues: from *"J'adore la neige"* to *"C'est trop beau."* Depth is not the least of Parisians' qualities.

When snow starts falling, everything stops in Paris. The city goes into a poetic blackout for one minute. Everyone just watches the snow fall with a smile. Hesitant between sheer melancholy and simple happiness.

Because sheer melancholy is too intimate and simple happiness is obviously a myth, Parisians quickly choose to pull themselves together. States of latency are not to persist for too long in Paris. Life is too serious for latency. The Parisian will take control over his emotions. At this point comes the litany of talks on how snow ends up being dirty because of all the cars and pollution.

All the smart talking about how it's interesting that *in banlieue*, it's usually colder so snow actually sticks, while in Paris it does not.

These conversations have no goal other than allowing the Parisian to brush the disruption of snow out of his life.

Opening up to emotion is a slippery slope for Parisians.

USEFUL TIP: Starting a snowball fight is only acceptable during the previously exposed moment of latency. After this, it would be childish.

SOUND LIKE A PARISIAN: *J'aime trop la neige . . . ça me donne envie d'aller au ski.* ("I love snow so much . . . makes me want to go out to the mountain and ski.")

The Luxembourg Garden

The Luxembourg Garden (le Jardin du Luxembourg) is every Parisian's favorite park.

Along with Central Park, it is actually every Parisian's favorite park in the world.

Walking the alleys of *le Luco* is an enchantment for every Parisian.

Because the Luxembourg Garden is a delightfully elegant park, the style and peace of which he can appreciate, the Parisian feels a direct tie with Marie de Médicis when he's there. Walking the alleys of the park, the Parisian becomes royalty. People inside of whom the bells of monarchy fail to ring will most likely celebrate silently the great French democracy, embodied by *le Sénat,* magnanimous enough a representative body to let the good people of Paris enjoy its private gardens. The Luxembourg Garden, in a soft whirlwind of green, unites monarchists and *républicains.*

Besides this taste of the greatness of French history he now fully feels a part of, the Parisian also feels that a promenade in the Luxembourg is a journey in his personal story. Many personal memories come to the Parisian's mind when he enters the park. Memories of the time spent there as a student ditching classes, with a pretty girl he was courting back in the day or simply reading philosophy on his own, seated on one of the benevolent metal chairs. No bad memories can ever be associated with the Luxembourg. For the Parisian, the Luxembourg magnifies yesterday. It alters it, too. Needless to say, most Parisians did not skip classes and never read philosophy—ever.

Besides these beautiful reminiscences, the Luxembourg Garden is also a fantastically comforting place for the Parisian.

Outsiders think the Luxembourg Garden is just a park. But the Luxembourg Garden is actually a runway. The models of this runway are Parisians. An Enchanting show that is.

Three types one may find in the Luxembourg are people walking, people jogging, and people seated. Walkers are of

two varieties: Parisians and tourists. Parisians walking in *le Luco* usually live nearby. Most are from a rich and powerful extraction. Much elegance ensues. Joggers are incongruous in this environment. They run around the park frenetically. Two types of joggers: Parisians and expats. Parisians jogging in the Luxembourg Gardens are usually local yuppies trying to turn the Luxembourg Gardens into the Central Park of Paris. People seated are also either Parisians or expats (tourists are too busy for sitting). They like to pretend they are reading. Truth is, they are sunbathing and people watching. Seated males also fall in love with the mysteriously evanescent Parisian girls walking there.

In the end, the Luxembourg Garden is a necessary respite and an absolute continuation of the life and activities of the Rive Gauche.

In that it talks to the mind of the *promeneur*, le Jardin du Luxembourg epitomizes what nature really is about in Paris: a fresh and soft stroke on the Parisian's mind.

USEFUL TIP: It is a necessity to know what the current *expo photo au Luxembourg* is about. Always.

SOUND LIKE A PARISIAN: *On va se balader au Luxembourg, j'ai besoin d'être à l'air libre!* ("Let's take a stroll at Luxembourg, I need fresh air!")

Calling People by Their License Plate

Not being from Paris happens.

Yet, the Parisian rarely holds anyone responsible for not being from Paris. Though he will surely believe that the root of any mistake the non-Parisian makes is to be found in his suspicious origins. This tendency is particularly true for any interaction that implicates an automobile.

The moment a non-Parisian sits in a car, he becomes the last two digits of his license plate. Immediately. He becomes *un 78, le 42,* or *un 29.* The last two digits of a French license plate correspond to that of the *département* of registration of the car. Paris is 75. Other numbers smell like mud or depression.

Numbers that smell like mud are the rare numbers. The ones you hardly ever see on the streets of Paris. Those are 07, 86, 41, 23, 53. . . . Mud somewhat recalls the Parisian of some remote vacation spot. Mud is not always bad. *Le 07* for instance will take too much time on the road, he will hesitate, he will let pedestrians cross the street. He is obviously *un paysan.* But the Parisian has a certain affection for him. So he will be merciful. Lenient. That is how people of the city should be, really.

The rest of the numbers smell like depression. Areas supposedly colder or less sunny than Paris, obviously. But more commonly: *la banlieue.* Anyone walking the streets of Paris should know that *les 77, les 78, les 91, les 92, les 93, les 94,* and *les 95* are from *la banlieue,* which implies that they have limited self-esteem, minimal respect for others, and an awful dose of rawness to them. These people are a direct threat on the road. Out of *la banlieue* numbers, two rank higher up in the Parisian's hierarchy of numbers: 78 and 92. These two *départements* include very fancy towns and expensive neighborhoods. Less shameful.

Traffic in Paris seems hectic to the occasional visitor. Yet it does follow very simple rules.

Rule number one: pedestrians do not exist.

Rule number two: congestions are always caused by mud numbers. *C'est ce con de 27 qui bloque tout le monde depuis deux heures.* ("Some idiot from 27 has been blocking everyone for two hours.")

Rule number three: any outrageous driving is always caused by depression numbers: *Mais il est complètement con le 94. Il va*

tuer quelqu'un. ("This 94 is a complete idiot. He's going to kill someone.")

It is obvious knowledge that 75s have superior driving skills. They do live in Paris after all.

Ultimately, knowing about the origin of a fellow driver helps the Parisian anticipate the flaws of his driving style. He therefore constantly bears in mind that he will only be safe surrounded by 75s. Thus making Paris the only place on earth where people act on the road exactly as they do off it.

USEFUL TIP: Learn your *départements*.

SOUND LIKE A PARISIAN: *Non, mais c'est ce con de 72 qui fait chier son monde!* ("This 72 retard is getting on everyone's nerves!")

Jeans

Finding the age of a Parisian is easy.

All Parisians under fifty years old always wear jeans. All Parisians over fifty years old never wear jeans.

Jeans is the new Parisian uniform. Not wearing jeans in Paris is pure subversion.

Parisian men love their jeans, for they are a fantastic means to make a strong social statement. For those of them who wear suits at work, fun time is chill time: weekend is therefore jeans time. Regular pants would remind them of work too much. Jeans really are about freedom. So is the weekend.

For all Parisian men who do not need to wear suits at work, jeans are a shouting way to stress it. "I am no slave to the system: I work in jeans." These Parisians have managed to turn jean wearing into an act of pure arrogance. Parisians really are brilliant.

Women also wear jeans. Constantly. While Parisian men usually own two or three pairs, it is frequent for Parisian women to own up to ten pairs of jeans. When it comes to choosing a pair of jeans, Parisian women only ask themselves one question: *Est-ce qu'il me fait un gros cul?* ("Does it make my ass look big?") Yes, Parisian women can be rude like that. While Parisian men tend to stick to blue jeans, Parisian women do not hesitate to broaden their horizons, wearing black and occasionally gray. Style is about daring, isn't it?

As with every uniform, wearing jeans comes with a few rules.

Rule number one is that jeans are never to be worn with sneakers in Paris. A person walking the streets of Paris wearing jeans and New Balance shoes is American. The only exception to that rule is Converse shoes. This exception works for both genders. Converse and jeans are OK in Paris. Rule number two of jeans wearing is what could be called the Diesel controversy. Wearing Diesel jeans sends out a message that the wearer is OK with spending 300 euros (U.S.$400) on a pair of jeans. And he's happy to throw that piece of information in your face. Which, of course, will make him the target of much talk, much to his delight.

Tucking in or not tucking in the shirt becomes the final assertion of one's personality. For men, collared shirts ought to be tucked in. Always. T-shirts and polo shirts ought not to be. Ever. For women, tucking in is always a bad idea.

Reaching a form of happiness in Paris implied internalizing certain codes and refusing certain habits. Thus, Parisians will always refuse not to wear jeans, as they will refuse to wear short-sleeved shirts. These two rules are milestones of contemporary Paris's defining moral system.

USEFUL TIP: The cut of your jeans will tell much about your sexual orientations and availability. Be cautious.

SOUND LIKE A PARISIAN: *Faut qu'j'm'achète un jean.* ("I need to buy some jeans.")

Berthillon

The best ice cream in the world is made in Paris. Of course.

And it can be found at Berthillon. Parisians of all social classes know about Berthillon. Parisians of all social classes have tasted Berthillon.

Berthillon is one of the rare forms of luxury all Parisians can afford.

The beauty of Berthillon lies in the outstanding quality of its *glaces et sorbets.* But the Berthillon experience goes beyond the tasty delights they offer.

The Berthillon experience starts with a line. There is no touching a Berthillon *cône glacé* without standing in line for at least a few seconds or a few minutes. The line gives the Parisian the occasion to choose the flavors and the number of *boules.* One is usual. Two is for *les gourmands.*

Anything beyond two is for *les Américains.*

Once served, it is usual for the Parisian to go for a little stroll on l'Ile Saint-Louis with his *glace.* The Parisian will systematically ask his co-Berthilloner, *C'est bon?* His is always *super bon.*

The Berthillon experience is vastly enhanced by the localization of Berthillon shops and resellers—exclusively on l'Ile Saint-Louis. Tasting a *glace* Berthillon is the only time the Parisian is happy to behave exactly like a tourist. Outside of that occurrence, it is a disgrace.

There is a form of pride in having Berthillon. Buying a *glace* Berthillon makes you all at once very gourmet, very distinguished, very in the know, very old school, and very rich. Every time he stops at Berthillon for ice cream, the Parisian will tell all the people he meets for the rest of the week. *On s'est arrêtés chez Berthillon.* Perfect name-dropping.

The other Parisians will be jealous: Berthillon is the gift that keeps giving.

With the surge over the past decades of American and Italian ice cream chains, Berthillon has a lot of competition.

By opting for a small family-owned business that has never branched out or started selling ice cream in supermarkets or overseas, Parisians unconsciously know that by buying *des glaces* Berthillon, they do more than just treat themselves with a *petit plaisir*: they support a certain form of civilization. A certain idea of the world. A certain idea of Paris.

USEFUL TIP: Come at night: Berthillon, Notre Dame, and l'Ile Saint-Louis under the Parisian skies are an irresistible combination.

SOUND LIKE A PARISIAN: *Berthillon?! Eh bah ça, va, tu te fais plaisir!* ("Berthillon?! Look at you, Mr. Gourmet!")

Roland Garros

All Parisians love Roland Garros.

Not the man—the tennis tournament. Known overseas as the French Open. Roland Garros is all good news for Parisians.

First, it means spring has arrived. Roland Garros is the official kick-off of the best months of the year. The French Open is allegedly a tennis tournament. Truth be told, it is Paris's prime solarium. Parisians go to Roland Garros first and foremost to sunbathe.

Besides its tanning function, Roland Garros is one of the greatest social events in Paris. The beauty of Roland Garros lies in the fact that it is both completely exclusive and completely open. Whether one partakes in the exclusive or in the generic experience, he can still brag with his friends: *J'étais à Roland Garros hier.* The evocation of Roland Garros comes with a beautiful touch of glamour and Parisian elegance. VIPs and corporate guests are allowed inside *le Village.* The plebe will stick to *les Allées.* Corporate snobs only spend two or three hours *à Roland.* A sunny and extended lunch break.

Once seated in *le Central,* Parisians' attention is hardly focused on tennis. Sure, they need to keep track of the score for future reference, but the real quest is to spot celebrities. Parisians find quite sweet the feeling of casually sharing hobbies and experiences with celebrities.

One of the things Parisians love about Roland Garros is that it's situated on the outskirts of Paris in the beautiful Bois de Boulogne. Meaning, as opposed to many other sporting events, it does not screw up their lives by worsening traffic. There is really nothing bad about Roland Garros.

In late May, Paris is split into two categories of people: those who have tickets for *la finale,* and everyone else. The first type is considered *salauds* by the second. The ticket possessors secretly agree and giggle in petto: they made it in life.

When going to Roland Garros, it is acceptable for Parisians to buy a souvenir. T-shirts or towels are the most frequent choice. Tennis balls are also OK. While buying a branded souvenir from any other place they visit would be considered outrageously *beauf,* it is absolutely OK with Roland Garros gear. So is buying ice cream to enjoy while watching the games. Even for Parisian women . . .

Spring's high mass finally allows pleasure. Everything suddenly seems to become possible, passed the *périphérique.*

USEFUL TIP: Bring sunscreen.

SOUND LIKE A PARISIAN: *Tu vas à Roland Garros? Oooh, trop d'la chance.* ("You're going to Roland Garros? Oooh, so lucky!")

Old Friends

Parisians are happy with their friends.

They do not need new friends.

By the age of twenty-three, Parisians have found all their friends for life.

Parisians have three groups of friends: childhood friends, friends from high school, and friends from college. Add a handful of friends they met on vacations and the one or two remaining from the countless hours they spent as kids at sports or music practice and you'll have it all. Among these, the actual main group of friends is the college friends. Other friends are kind of a chore to see.

It is important to realize that most Parisians are tired of most of their friends. Hence, a natural defiance against new friends. They will probably be tired of them soon as well. Why bother?

Newcomers to Paris can therefore only befriend Parisians of age twenty-three and under. If aiming older, only *provinciaux* and foreigners will be available. The only way to make Parisian friends is to start a relationship with a person that has befriended Parisians when they were younger than twenty-three. This will grant you the honor of their company.

When entering this prestigious circle, you will be a disruptive element in a group that has most likely been static for several years. This will be the source of much jealousy, drama, and talking. Excessive friendliness will be considered obscene flirtation. Be prepared to be hated by people of your gender or loved by people from the other. That is the rule of new interactions with Parisians.

Old friends give Parisians a strong sense of grounding that they feel urban life deprived them of. Sticking to their friends also gives Parisians a real sense of comfort. By knowing their friends inside and out, they infer that they know the world inside and out. Given such striking deductive talent, no one can really blame Parisians for their shortcomings, when it comes to adding new friends to their life.

USEFUL TIP: Don't bother! *Provinciaux* tend to be more fun anyway.

SOUND LIKE A PARISIAN: *Je dîne avec Guillaume jeudi. Pff, ca me saoule, mais j'ai déjà annulé deux fois, il faut vraiment qu'j'y aille.* ("I'm eating with Guillaume on Thursday. I really don't want to go but I already canceled on him twice before, so I really have to.")

Seine River Cruises

Parisians are dreamers. La Seine is their ocean.

Seine River cruises are their odyssey.

Parisians have a deep love for the Seine. Love in Paris is tender but fierce, therefore all Parisians find the Seine both incredibly beautiful and completely *dégueulasse.*

Criticism never hurts. Especially a river.

A Seine River cruise is an emotionally loaded moment for every Parisian. It brings back childhood memories of the usual *sortie de classe* on the Bateaux-Mouches (yes, the Parisian was once a child). Memories of his teen years when bringing his provincial cousin on a Seine River cruise was the worst imaginable chore. Memories of his student years when he grasped that the beauty of his city was his major asset to ever seal his romantic endeavors and finally discover physical pleasures (true, the Parisian is no early bloomer). Seine River cruises are always striking moments in the life of the Parisian.

Yet, Seine River cruises are one of these things the Parisian likes without knowing or admitting he does. The only thing the Parisian is able to say when hearing the phrase *"Croisière sur la Seine"* is *"C'est un truc de touristes."*

Nothing is more degrading for the Parisian than doing *des trucs de touristes.* But the Parisian has a good heart. So one day, as a grown-up, he will take his Spanish friends, his children, his clients, or his mistress on a cruise along the Seine.

While on the boat, the Parisian will always stand outside—with his collar popped. Inside is for suckers. The Parisian likes to feel the wind, the sun, the brutality of the elements whipping his face.

The Seine becomes his Bermuda Triangle.

Such is the Parisian, fearless and adventurous.

USEFUL TIP: To spot the Parisians on a Seine River cruise, just look for people wearing sailing jackets.

SOUND LIKE A PARISIAN: *J'ai fait une croisière sur la Seine l'autre jour. Il f'sait hyper beau—c'était hyper sympa.* ("I took a cruise on the Seine the other day. It was beautiful out—really good fun.")

Wearing Black

Paris is the city of fashion. Especially if fashion consists of wearing black. Parisians love to wear black: black pants, black shoes, black coats, you name it.

Parisian women are especially fond of black clothes. It is well known that *le noir, ça mincit.* Parisian women have a mild obsession with looking thin, and so black is their best friend.

But besides its fantastic fat-erasing skills, black is a priceless social color in Paris. With black, you go unnoticed.

Going unnoticed is the dream of every Parisian. The Parisian does not want his clothes to reveal his singularity. The only singularity worth revealing in Paris is that of the mind. Therefore the Parisian's clothes ought to be simple: all Parisians know that *le noir, c'est simple, c'est bien.* ("Black is simple; it's good.")

The Parisian knows his colors. Parisians look at people dressed colorfully with a fair bit of disdain.

Style exuberance in Paris is considered offensive.

The mental sanity of a person bold enough to wear such outrageous colors as yellow or red will be questioned at once by all Parisians. There is no wearing red or yellow in Paris if you are mentally sane. Blue is acceptable. Especially navy blue, which has the good taste of being easily mistaken for black.

The golden rule of black wearing has only one exception,

and that is a seasonal one. In the summertime, Parisian guys get to wear white. For *le blanc, c'est simple, c'est bien.* ("White is simple; it's good.")

Parisian girls will opt for *la couleur de l'été.* Every summer comes with a new official color dictated by women's magazines. Color originality has its limits.

All Parisian girls happily accept this new seasonal paradigm. Walking in the streets of Paris on a "blue" summer feels like walking through an urban Smurf village.

When the Parisian boyfriend points out the ugliness of the color, the Parisian girlfriend systematically looks at him with a mix of desperation and exasperation. *C'est hyper tendance cette couleur cet été, tu comprends rien.* ("That color is so hip this summer, you just don't get it.")

Indeed, Parisian men could make an effort: that was a simple one.

USEFUL TIP: Do not wear black only. A white collar is always an elegant—and simple—addition.

SOUND LIKE A PARISIAN: *J' me suis acheté un p'tit pull noir, tout simple, super mignon . . .* ("I just bought a small black coat, simple and cute . . .")

Having Theories

Thinking differently in Paris does not imply radical or in-depth questionings. Thinking differently simply implies appearing to be thinking differently. In Paris, this takes the form of having theories.

Parisians have an opinion about most things, thus making it clear they have a significant knowledge about most things in life.

Having theories takes this to the next level. Theories prove that not only does the Parisian have more information and knowledge than other people, but he also processed that information through his own personal filter. The superiority filter.

Parisians have theories about everything and everyone. They do, though, have a special liking for theories that revolve around politics. By politics, the Parisian intends two things: intense battles for power and politicians' sex lives.

Coming up with blunt media-ingested-type information is a sign of mental weakness in Paris. To come up with a good theory, the Parisian needs to connect facts that are usually not connected or that bring new elements to the table. It is important to appear to be doing this in an intelligent manner. Theories are all about shedding a new light. Parisians create the light.

To introduce his theories, the Parisian will usually use one of two introductory clauses: *j'ai ma théorie* usually works for theories about people but shows that the theory is not really a serious one; *j'ai une théorie* shows others that some serious thinking has been put into it and others will listen, for their intellect has been turned on by this expression. But the most Machiavellian Parisians will use theory after theory but never warn that these are theories. Other people, including Parisians, will be fooled and will inevitably reach the conclusion that this Parisian is extremely *cultivé* and intelligent.

It is important to realize that very few Parisians form their own theories. Most Parisians repeat theories they heard on TV, or from their really smart uncle. No credit is ever given to the actual source. The actual source is always the Parisian.

When a theory has become repeated so much that it stops being a catchy theory in Paris, Parisians usually refrain from using it, for they do not want to come across as fake theory people. They will nonetheless recycle these old theories when they go *en province.*

For obviously, Parisians have a theory about *provinciaux*: they have no clue.

USEFUL TIP: Use theories with parsimony, at the risk of appearing as an adept of conspiracy theories, which is a brutal form of disgrace in Paris.

SOUND LIKE A PARISIAN: *Moi j'ai une théorie: les gens qui portent des pantalons à pince . . .* ("I have a theory about men who wear pants with apparent folds on each leg . . .")

Les Grandes Écoles

In Paris, academic performance is the main—if not the only—determinant of intelligence. Consequently, people who did graduate from a *grande école* are considered superior beings.

Faire de bonnes études in France means only two things: *faire médecine* or *faire une grande école*. All the rest is crap.

Les grandes écoles are a highly competitive set of graduate schools. They fall into two categories: *commerce* (ESSEC, HEC) and *ingénieur* (Polytechnique, Centrale, Mines, Ponts). Add Sciences Po (which is halfway through) and Ulm (which is not properly *une école*) to that list and there you have your French *grandes écoles*. Conveniently, they are all based in the surroundings of Paris. (Where else?)

Graduating from a *Grande École* leaves in the Parisian subconscious mind a more lasting mark than a tattoo on a Finn's skin. Most Parisians who did not graduate from a *grande école* consequently feel a form of discomfort about it. They might be great parents, great professionals, or great people, but they missed that key milestone of Parisian intelligence.

It is therefore every Parisian's dream to have at least one of his children entering a *grande école*. If that happens, the Parisian can die in peace.

The fact that a person is a student or an alumnus of a *grande école* usually comes early in a conversation. Rarely though from

the actual graduate: more frequently, this piece of information is brought to the table by the inferior friend, who is too happy to boast a *grande école* friend in front of his other inferior friends: *"J'étais là-bas avec Marc, tu sais, mon copain centralien . . ."* At this point, the *grande école* graduate adopts a humble "I'm just like you guys" profile. On top of being smarter, he is also *sympa*. This makes others admire him even more.

Grandes écoles are hard to get into. It takes excellent grades, hard work, educated parents, and a hint of luck. The most fantastic thing about putting together that combination is that no matter what he does with his life, Parisians will always consider the *grande école* graduate to be superior. And therefore entitled throughout his career.

The fact that most *grande école* graduates end up being gray corporate executives is not relevant. Their intelligence has been vouched already. They won. Everybody else lost. It is important to realize that in Paris, no successful entrepreneur, artist, writer, chef, or artisan can be considered part of the elite (at least in his lifetime). This category is exclusively reserved to *grandes écoles* alumni. Other people are expected to move on.

By understanding that intelligence is onefold and fully determined at age twenty, Parisians manage to offer the world an easily readable social scale. Finally! *Merci qui?*

USEFUL TIP: The most obvious form of professional success in Paris is to be a *grande école* almunus's boss.

SOUND LIKE A PARISIAN: *Tu sais que Diane se marie?! Un garçon très bien, ESSEC, super sympa.* ("You know who Diane is marrying? A great guy, ESSEC graduate, really nice.")

Despising le PSG

In Paris, the ultimate form of mental degradation is to support a sports team.

Parisians are not into sports very much. Playing sports is degrading. Watching sports on TV is straight-up shameful.

Yet the Parisian is an understanding person. He will give his friend an earful if the friend said he watched *du foot à la télé* the night before. But he understands. What he does not understand and therefore does not tolerate is the act of supporting one given sports team.

Blind and continuous support to a cause is fully acceptable in Paris should the cause be a social or political one. Blind and continuous support to any other cause should be treated with nothing but contempt. This rule applies to all people within Paris.

Though it is worthwhile to know that Parisians find a certain romantic appeal to soccer/football fanatics in Marseille, in Lens, and in Latin countries. All other soccer fans are irremediable *beaufs*.

The most repelling form of degradation in Paris is to support the local soccer/football team: le Paris Saint-Germain (aka le PSG). It is obvious Parisian knowledge that there is nothing good about le PSG. Nothing.

Consequently, there can be nothing good about PSG fans.

Not only are they sports fans, they are soccer fans. Not only are they soccer fans, they are PSG fans. A hopeless category of people.

The only Parisians who like le PSG are *banlieusards* ("suburbanites"). *Banlieusards* thus feel like they actually are Parisians. Needless to say, this is foolishly illusory. No one who grew up or lives on the other side of *le périphérique*, no matter how close, can ever claim, one day, to be a Parisian.

The hatred against le PSG is so deeply rooted in Parisians that simply going to le Parc des Princes to see a game is considered a social disgrace. Interestingly, while going to see a PSG game is the most obvious form of absence of dignity in Paris, it is fully acceptable, if not cool, to go see le Stade Français—Paris's rugby team. Parisians are people of taste. Rugby cannot be compared to soccer.

The Parisian feels great about hating le PSG. By doing so, he clearly states that he is not a *beauf*, not into sports, and not blinded by illusory feelings of belonging. Hating le PSG is just another oblivious statement of superiority for Parisians. In hatred, the Parisian grows as a person.

USEFUL TIP: Buying a PSG jersey is a great gift for anyone who lives outside Europe. Europeans prefer a Stade Français item.

SOUND LIKE A PARISIAN: *Tu vois le mec, ambiance, genre, euh . . . supporter du PSG!* ("The guy was like . . . hmm . . . PSG-fan type!")

Diets

Parisians are all too fat. They are therefore all on a diet.

After the weather conversation, the weight conversation is the Parisian's favorite. It is a fantastic conversation. It allows the Parisian to display his observation talent and his contrition while at the same time showing ambition and resolution.

The Parisian will not let fatness take over.

Comments about the weight gained or lost by a person—should that person be facing the Parisian or not—are usual and widely accepted. Being utterly sensitive, the Parisian frequently enriches his weight comments with psychological explanations. The most common reason in Paris to explain weight gain is *il a pas trop la forme* ("he's kind of down these days"). The Parisian knows how to play with words. Psychological contributions aim at displaying a deeper level of consciousness and a real sense of empathy. The Parisian never sees you as just a body. The Parisian knows you are first and foremost a soul.

Only one expression can precede weight comments. That is *bah dis donc*: *Bah dis donc, t'as pris un peu, non?!* Or, the reverse, *Bah dis donc, t'as vachement maigri.* It is good to know that the Parisian will only seem to rejoice about a friend's weight loss. Deep inside, all he thinks about is that his weight is not following the same noble curve.

A common mistake is to believe that only Parisian women are dieting. Men are, too. Paris is the only city in the world where men eat salads for lunch. It would be misleading to draw conclusions about the salad-eating Parisian man's sexual orientation.

Diets in Paris are not followed in a precise manner. Especially by men. In Paris, social life undermines all possibilities of an actual diet. Hence all possibilities of an actual weight loss. Since diets do not work, Parisians need more diets. Parisian women try diets they hear about in magazines or from their friends. Parisian men just skip dessert. Yet Parisian men are never *au régime*, Parisian men *font gaffe en ce moment.* It is not the same.

Parisians cannot get enough of *allégé*, "0 percent," and "light" mentions on the foods they buy. It has lately become unthinkable for Parisian women to buy yogurts that are not 0 percent.

While the rest of the world wants more for less, the Parisian wants less for more. Diets in Paris are the path to wisdom.

USEFUL TIP: Compliment Parisian men about their weight losses. They will pretend not to care. But you and I know better.

SOUND LIKE A PARISIAN: *Un p'tit dessert? Non, j'fais gaffe en c'moment.* ("A little dessert? No, I'm being careful these days.")

Knowing About Current Exhibits

Art exhibits are a Parisian must. They are many and constant. Modern art, photographers, retrospectives . . . you name it. Most Parisians are aware of the main *expos* going on.

It would yet be naive to believe that the point for Parisians to know about current exhibits is to go see them or to develop their culture. The real point of knowing about current exhibits is to show you know about current exhibits. The main effect of which will be an immediate increase in the Parisian's perceived social value.

Knowing about current *expos*, if displayed frequently yet rather discreetly, will make Parisians seem delightfully refined and cultured. Parisians show reverence to people of culture.

It is important to understand that ultimate levels of sophistication do not come in Paris from being a person of culture but from coming across as one. Culture is a fool's game in Paris. One may think that keeping up with the ever-changing new *expo* scene is a lot of work. Again, it is not. Remember, it is not about knowing but about looking like you do. Many Parisians pass a museum on their way to work every morning. And the current main exhibit is always massively advertised in the Metro or on the streets. So right there, the Parisian can effortlessly fuel conversations with at least two exhibits people "need to see." Maximal effect will be achieved when, alongside with the artist, the Parisian also mentions where the exhibit is held. That is the highest form of culture in Paris.

It is basic Parisian knowledge that only six categories of people go to art exhibits in Paris. They are *provinciaux*, foreign exchange students, teachers, foreign tourists, retirees, and expats' wives. No other Parisian has ever seen an *expo* ever.

Yet all Parisians always "really want to go see it.' Usually because they "heard it was great." Sadly, they "really don't have time." But just in case, they'll ask, "When does it end?"

While figuring out this pernicious Parisian approach to cultural life, non-Parisians may think "name-dropping." Foolish. It's art-dropping. Art-dropping creates an artsy feeling all around. Contagious bubbles of art talk flourish throughout the city. Experts fail to comment on it, but make no mistake: art-dropping will soon be considered a form of art itself.

By neglecting art, Parisians create art.

USEFUL TIP: Only say you actually went to see *une expo* when talking to people from one of the six categories mentioned above. It would be rude and pretentious to do so with a Parisian.

SOUND LIKE A PARISIAN: *Il y a une super expo Avedon en ce moment au Jeu de Paume.* ("There is a super exhibit on Avedon right now at Jeu de Paume.")

Scruffs

Parisian men are not to shave every day. Parisian men are to have a scruff.

A good scruff sends Parisian men to the very top of the sexiness scale. Men with a scruff are somewhere between Indiana Jones in Malaysia and George Clooney on a Sunday afternoon. Scruff makes Parisian men irresistible.

Parisian men want to be irresistible.

Parisian women love their men with a scruff. They love this itchy expression of adventure that grows on their men's faces. A scruff offers Parisians just the right dose of adventure. Civilized adventure. The look of adventure without the smell of it. Potential is more than enough in Paris.

In Paris, having a scruff is a social affirmation. A man with a scruff in not a tool of the corporate world. Scruff is a clear indication of freedom in Paris. The more high end the place the Parisian man goes with a scruff, the more powerful and confident he obviously is. The limit of scruff wearing is pushed a bit further every day in Paris.

Though they love their scruff, Parisian men must go about saying they are tired of their scruff. They need to bitch about how they need to shave and how shaving is such an oppressive task. Parisian men will always shave before meeting up with their mother. It is obviously Parisian knowledge that to Parisian mothers, a scruffy son is a terrible thing.

Scruff experts do not shave with a razor, but with a *tondeuse.* Use of *la tondeuse* allows the most advanced Parisian men to keep a permanent *barbe de trois jours.* With a bit of aesthetic talent and a sense of facial hair styling, Parisian men achieve this miracle, making three days last forever.

With just a scruff, Parisian men manage to attract women, express their inalienable freedom, and stop time. Yet their day hasn't even started yet. Now who can beat *that*?

USEFUL TIP: Scruff with very elegant clothes is the absolute key to success in Paris.

SOUND LIKE A PARISIAN: *Ouais, faut qu'j'me rase.* ("Yeah, I need to shave.")

Version Originale (V.O.)

In Paris, foreign movies are to be watched in *V.O.* (*V.O.* stands for *version originale*—which means in their language of origin, with French subtitles.)

If you watch a foreign film in *V.F.* (*version française*), you are a *beauf.* Straight up.

Watching a movie in *V.O.* allows the Parisian to display his superiority in many ways. First off, if the Parisian does so, it is because he is a fantastic English speaker (a huge number of foreign films played in France are American or British). Whether or not the Parisian actually speaks English is irrelevant. He watches films *en V.O.* so he is.

Besides being talented and obviously well traveled, the Parisian is also quite the culture person. Therefore he will not tolerate for a work of art to be butchered by poorly executed voice-overs. *V.O.* is just better. This is not a valid point for Asian movies though.

It is OK to butcher Asian movies with poorly executed voice-overs.

If you want to make your Parisian friend feel good about himself, simply offer him the opportunity to watch a movie in *V.F.* He will refuse with much seriousness, arguing that he never watches movies in *V.F.* Ever. *Je ne supporte pas* ("I can't stand it") is usually the response you will get. The Parisian just drowned you in the deep seas of ignorance and disdain. Very satisfying feeling. Well done on your side: you just strengthened your friendship with the Parisian.

The Parisian's love for *V.O.* now goes beyond movie theaters. In Paris, it is no longer acceptable to like American TV shows in *V.F.* A few precursors started the trend a decade ago with the show *Friends*: *Je supporte pas la voix de Ross en français.* ("I cannot stand Ross's voice in French.") Most Parisians just cannot cope any more with the dubbed versions that TV plays these days. They need to buy the DVDs. It is an obligation. Intellectual excellence has its price.

Parisians are willing to pay that price.

USEFUL TIP: To look more Parisian, request *V.O.* It is evidence.

SOUND LIKE A PARISIAN: *V.F.? Pas moyen!* ("*V.F.?* No way!")

Doubts

Some may think that Parisians live in Paris. They don't.

They live in doubt.

Parisians doubt.

They doubt everything. All the time.

Truthfully, the Parisian mostly doubts good things. Bad things are rarely questioned, for the Parisian knows that bad is part of life.

Doubt is a structuring element of Parisian thinking. Doubt offers one of these double-win situations Parisians cannot get enough of. When doubting, you win because you are smarter. If you doubt, you question the given. You shed the higher and brighter light of your intelligence and experience on things.

But doubting is also a wonderful buffer against enthusiasm and its load of degrading positive vibes. Parisians will doubt any good news. Systematically. They will question the origin, the reality, or the outcome of any new fact. Being in an analytical state allows the Parisian to ingeniously dodge emotional states.

The Parisian is a thinker. Not a feeler. Cold states comfort him.

Doubting people will provide the Parisian with much less social gratification than doubting facts or situations. Doubting someone will be seen as a display of insecurity. It is not recommended. Parisians only doubt two types of people: their parents and their significant other. The Parisian only doubts the people he knows the most.

By doubting things in a systematic manner, the Parisian never expects anything good to come for him. If something good happens, the Parisian will be annoyed that his doubts did not end up being justified. If his doubts were justified and something bad happens, the Parisian will feel the thrill of success and intelligence down his spine.

Bad feels good for Parisians.

USEFUL TIP: The most common expression of doubt in Paris is nonverbal. Lip action.

SOUND LIKE A PARISIAN: *Mouais . . . ca m'étonnerait quand même!* ("Well . . . I do have my doubts about that really!")

Jacques Brel

Parisians want to be great and in pain.

Jacques Brel was great, and he was in pain.

Therefore Jacques Brel is every Parisian's idol.

Parisians reluctantly admit to seeing value in other human beings. Only a few can make it to the pantheon of Parisians' acceptance. Even fewer are artists. Jacques Brel was one of them.

Jacques Brel was Belgian. Usually, Parisians would hold that against him. But Brel's talent made him universal. And therefore ultimately Parisian.

Every Parisian believes deep inside that he has the talent to be a fantastic artist. Life turned out differently but the potential was there. The Parisian is lazy or caught up in life. But he is immensely talented. Brel was a fantastic artist: by excelling in song writing, singing, and interpretation, he kindly put a mirror in front of every Parisian's face. Every Parisian could be Jacques Brel. Every Parisian is Jacques Brel. At least the greatness of Jacques Brel.

Because Brel was also a man in pain. Scandalized by the brutalities of life. Brel was singing his pain away. Parisians are addicted to pain. They admire pain.

A man in pain got it.

His sulfurous combination of pain and talent, presented

with the luster of elegance and truthfulness, is a turn-on for every Parisian. In Paris, constant pain is a form of intellectual distinction. Brel turned pain into beauty. Parisians are forever thankful for that. Brel did not destroy the pain. He magnified it.

While engaging in a conversation about Brel with a Parisian, it is imperative to also mention Brassens. Brassens and Brel in Paris come as a package.

USEFUL TIP: A great present for a Parisian is the poster of Jacques Brel, George Brassens, and Léo Ferré. Definitely belongs in his *toilettes*.

SOUND LIKE A PARISIAN: *Brel, c'était le plus grand!* ("Brel was the greatest!")

Le Moelleux au Chocolat

Parisians are guilty by essence.

Guilt is a Parisian's closest companion.

Parisians like to feed their good old friend guilt. Unconsciously, most of the time. But even, at times, in a perversely conscious manner. The toy of choice for Parisians to pet their guilt is not sex. It is *le moelleux au chocolat. Le moelleux au chocolat* is pure indulgence. The ultimate form of chocolate-based pleasure. An irresistible mix of mostly chocolate, butter, and sin.

Parisians all love their *moelleux au chocolat.* Every restaurant in Paris carries a *moelleux*. It has become a Parisian obsession.

A discharge system for all frustrations. A deep hole to jump into blindly.

Le moelleux is dark, sweet, warm, and runny. It is an orgasm crowning Parisian dinners.

All Parisians feel bad about ordering their *moelleux*. Most usually handle guilt leaks at the moment of ordering it with a *"La vie est courte"* ("Life is short") or an *"Allez hop, un petit plaisir"* ("A little treat, come on"). Phrases Parisian men would surely like to hear more often.

Eden's garden had the apple, Paris has the *moelleux*.

Le moelleux is so synonymous with forbidden pleasure that most waiters now offer two spoons when the Parisian orders a *moelleux*. Against all odds, at that very moment, Parisian waiters become sympathetic. Their legendary coldness is broken down. The weight of guilt on the *moelleux* eater is too vertiginous. He needs help. He needs another spoon. Even the chef steps in by frequently adding vanilla ice cream on the plate. Foodies think the vanilla ice cream is a triumphant form of contrast, *chaud-froid* and black-white all at once, highlighting the brotherly insolence of the silky textures. But no. Vanilla ice cream is just there as a relief. It is just there to make the *moelleux* eater feel better about himself. Vanilla ice cream brings the lightness and the freshness. A spoonful of *glace vanille*, even mixed with a bite of *moelleux*, is still not *moelleux* all the way.

Le moelleux au chocolat is a very accurate emotional indicator. When witnessing someone eating a *moelleux*, it is imperative to be quite considerate and delicate with that person. *Moelleux* eaters indulge because they need to. *Le moelleux* is the French and fattening version of the American hug. These people are in pain. They need a quick fix. But the *moelleux*, by feeding their guilt, will only increase their pain. Niceness is necessary before, during, and after a *moelleux*.

Parisian women are known to be relentless *moelleux* eaters. On a date, an observant Parisian can easily anticipate the outcome of this forming relationship. If the girl opts for *le moelleux*, sexual misery will ensue. Parisian women are known not to indulge twice the same night. It will therefore come as no surprise that ever since the introduction of *le moelleux* in Parisian restaurants, sexual activity in Paris has plummeted.

USEFUL TIP: A restaurant with no *moelleux* on the menu is considered either very traditional or straight up avant-garde in Paris.

SOUND LIKE A PARISIAN: *On se prend un p'tit moelleux?* ("Care to share a little *moelleux*?")

100%
PARISIEN
APPROUVÉ

The Idea of Sailing

Parisians always have somewhere in their minds the idea of something greater.

Something endless.

Something far.

Parisians all have somewhere in their minds Baudelaire's line: *Homme Libre, toujours tu chériras la mer.* Their minds are filled with a faraway blue.

Parisians are all, deep inside, sailing the seven seas.

Sailing is something a Parisian cannot not like. Not liking sailing is a clear indication in Paris that you are deprived of a soul. Sailing is elegant and poetic. It is therefore Parisian.

Nothing impresses a Parisian more that someone who left everything to go sail around the world: this is every Parisian's vision of happiness. Some may argue that this form of happiness might be uncomfortable and wet. Such a lack of *grandeur d'âme* will forever discard you as an individual. Criticizing sailing is only permitted to one category of people: pretty girls who have actually been on a sailboat. They are the only ones entitled to say that sailing is humid, slow, and sometimes dangerous. That will comfort Parisian men in the belief of their intellectual and poetic superiority over their materialistic female counterpart. This will make Parisian men love these Parisian women even more.

Whether or not the Parisian actually sails is irrelevant. The idea of sailing is superior to the action of sailing. Besides, pretty Parisian girls are right, sailing is humid and slow. And sometimes dangerous. So a great alternative to sailing for Parisians is to display sailing gear. Wearing *des chaussures bateau, un caban,* or *une vareuse* in Paris (wearing them all at once is unacceptable—one item at a time, please) just means you are superior. And chances are, sometimes you cry looking at the ocean. There is no beating this.

Sailing is so present in the Parisian's mind that he needs to be surrounded with representations of the greatness of sailing in his own home. All decent Parisians will always have a *livre de photos* with sailing-related pictures in it. If a coffee table book is not applicable, look for a framed picture in the bedroom or a poster in the *toilettes.* Pictures of angry oceans and lighthouses are also acceptable. Scale models of sailboats do not belong in a Parisian apartment. They should exclusively be displayed in the Parisian's *maison de campagne.*

If one day a Parisian tells you that he sails, make sure as of that moment you introduce him to other Parisians as *un super marin* ("a great sailor"). Pure ego boost. Even though you are not a sailor, he will like you for being such a discerning person.

Yes. The Parisian is magnanimous.

Sailing makes you a better person.

USEFUL TIP: When wearing sailing gear in Paris, make sure it looks old and beat up. . . . After all, you've sailed the seven seas with it.

SOUND LIKE A PARISIAN: *J'ai un copain qui a fait une transat . . . un mec génial!* ("A friend of mine did a transatlantic race . . . a terrific guy!")

Winning Conversations

Conversations are to Paris what dance battles are to hip-hop: moments of truth, shortcuts to glory.

A conversation in Paris is both a scene and a battle. Parisians win conversations. That's what they do.

For non-Parisians, this habit may seem unpleasant. For Parisians, it's a mind workout. Some people play sudoku; Parisians converse. Sure enough, Parisians sometimes indulge in small talk. They do. After all, they are human beings. But small talking is not conversing.

Conversing in Paris is an activity with two strict rules. Rule number one is that a Parisian conversation can only tackle the following topics: politics, economy, or geostrategy. No other subject is acceptable. Vulgar. Rule number two is a state of mind. To converse like a Parisian, systematic opposition is necessary. If the Parisian is opposed to his fellow converser's point, it means he obviously knows more than he does. His opponent soon enough starts wondering if the Parisian's knowledge is endless. Well done, the Parisian is starting to destroy his opponent's confidence.

Winning conversations is a matter of dignity in Paris.

If you merely partake in a conversation, you are a loser. If you lose a conversation, you are humiliated. You need to win. It is a necessity. Therefore dirty strategies are wildly tolerated.

A dirty trick Parisians like to pull is to come up with figures. Statistics. Percentages.

Parisians love figures in their conversations. This is a hard blow for opponents to counter. There is usually no coming back. It is implicit Parisian knowledge that the figure you come up with need not be true. It only needs to be well presented ("The other day, I was reading a UN report that . . ."). Parisians cannot get enough of the deadly efficiency of the dirty statistics strategy. They use it at all stages of conversation: as a final blow, as a continuous flow, or as a way to counter the opponent's superior reasoning.

Parisians have a sense of aesthetic beauty in the intellectual *combat-à-mort* a good Parisian conversation ought to be. Many Parisians will therefore stand for a cause they absolutely do not believe in. Especially when the room is filled with consensus. Consensus is a turn-on for many Parisians. The opportunity to take on a whole group of people is rare but potentially extremely rewarding. If you win, you will be feared and revered. This is gold for a Parisian.

When talking to his socialist friends, the Parisian will systematically wage a fierce crusade against *les fonctionnaires,* criticizing relentlessly the inefficiency of French bureaucracy. When talking to his friends from America, the same Parisian will sing the praises of the wonderful *protection sociale* France offers, taking credit for and bragging about the admirable achievements of French public transportation or hospitals while showing obvious contempt for America's disgustingly individualistic society. . . .

Conversations about wars are also a great intellectual workout for Parisians. All Parisians are known to be completely pro-war and anti-war in Afghanistan. Depending on their audience.

In the occurrence where he needs to be pro and anti a certain subject a few days apart, it is of course fully acceptable for the Parisian to reuse his previous opponent's arguments.

Some may consider this duplicity.

In Paris, it's called brilliance.

USEFUL TIP: When completely ignorant about a certain topic, use the Parisian women's strategy and call others "party poopers" or "too serious."

SOUND LIKE A PARISIAN: *Je lisais récemment que plus de quarante-cinq mille espèces animales ont disparu au cours des vingt dernières années. . . .* ("Recently I read that forty-five thousand species of animals have disappeared over the past twenty years. . . .")

Foreign Girls

La Parisienne is a myth. Straight up.

Walking in fancy Paris neighborhoods, one will surely run into many pretty and elegant women. Granted. But what most foreigners do not know about Parisian women is that they all share the same objective in life. The same motto that guides every single one of their actions. And that is: not to be a slut.

The consequences of standing for such a noble cause are plenty. The most evident ones are absence of flirting, resolute absence of sex appeal, constant sobriety, no cleavage, and contempt for all women who do not stand for the same cause. . . . Throughout their twenties and thirties, most *Parisiennes* are in a relationship (which of course annihilates the concept of a singles scene in Paris). No matter how lame it is, a stable relationship is the best shield against being considered a slut.

At some point, though, their relationship comes to an end, usually when Parisian men get sick of begging their women for oral gratification. These breakups lead to very serious life questioning and to much experimentation that usually goes untold at family reunions.

Needless to say, this unilateral take on life plunges both Parisian men and women into a very deep sexual misery.

Thankfully, Paris is a beautiful city.

A quick peak inside a Parisian bar will give you a good indication of how love works in the City of Love. A traditional bar in Paris will be 75 percent guys, 22 percent foreign girls, and a handful of French girls on the loose (usually just accompanying their boyfriends). In bars, Parisian men discover an unsuspected reality: foreign girls are different. They can dance. They drink. They have fun.

There is usually no coming back.

Examples of illustrious Frenchmen ending up with foreign women are plenty: our current president (Italian) and prime minister (Welsh), Vincent Cassel (Italian), Olivier Martinez (not quite sure). . . . Proving that even for Parisian men with wealth, charm, and power, foreign women are, really, the way to go.

USEFUL TIP: When you like a *Parisienne*, stop liking her—it will make her like you.

SOUND LIKE A PARISIENNE: *Pfff*. . .

The Word *Petit*

Parisians are exquisitely delicate people. In Paris, big is not beautiful. Big is vulgar.

Offensive to Parisians' obvious refinement.

In Paris, anything plentiful is necessarily in excess. This applies to all fields. And especially to pleasurable elements of life, such as food, sun, fun . . . In Paris, a lot of pleasure is surely too much pleasure.

So, to keep their conscience clean, when designating a pleasurable indulgence, Parisians commonly precede it with the adjective *petit*.

Petit in French means "small" or "little." It doesn't carry the positive demeanor that you find in women's clothing sections of American department stores. *Petit* is just the opposite of "big." It conveys images of simplicity, moderation, cheapness, and conviviality. It is therefore a handy compliment for Parisians to designate their pleasurable activities. A way to relieve the discomfort that pleasure causes in their minds. Parisians are not into the grandiosity of life. They are the impressionists of entertainment. One *petite* brushstroke at a time.

There are countless examples of this staid mentality: Parisians are very keen to meet their friends for *un p'tit restau, une p'tite bière, une p'tite blanquette de veau, une p'tite soirée,* or *un p'tit ciné.* The adjective *petit* is used regardless of the greatness of work or expectations that the Parisian put into the experience or of the pleasure derived from it. The Parisian will never admit putting any sort of work in the preparation of anything pleasurable. Neither will he ever admit to expecting much from it.

The word *petit* is a double win for Parisians. Not only does it relieve their guilty conscience, but it also helps them assert their superiority.

Pleasure is a passive thing in Paris. A bonus. And the bonus will always be a little one. For Parisians, life is always already great. Any positive addition can only be a minor one. And the Parisian intends for you to know it.

To pet the Parisian's ego, ask him questions about his *p'tit weekend.* At this point, he will usually come up with a list of the fantastic things he did over the weekend in a very absent and non-enthusiastic manner ("went heli-skiing, then chilled by the pool, and then had dinner at this two-star restaurant"). Thus implicitly stating that his *p'tits weekends* are much greater than your great ones.

Parisians are superior to you. Just don't fight it.

USEFUL TIP: Similarly, painful or unpleasant experiences ought to be preceded by the adjective *gros*.

SOUND LIKE A PARISIAN: *Je vais vous demander une petite signature?* ("Can I ask you for a little signature, please?")

Making Lists

Parisians are beings of culture. And of power.

As such, Parisians like to impose their cultural superiority.

An insidious way for Parisians to do so is by making lists. While other human beings make lists of things they have to do, Parisians make lists of things they know.

Such lists may sound useless. And they would be if Parisians were not gracious enough to share them with others. Many sentences in Paris will be ended by a list, a quick enumeration: a discreet display of knowledge. Eastern Europe economy is booming? The Parisian will enlighten others with a "Totally, yeah. Poland, Estonia, Ukraine, it's crazy . . . completely booming."

At this point, you would embarrass the Parisian for thanking him for this element of culture he brings to the table. He is being delicate and considerate with you and would appreciate equal courtesy from you in return.

Some argue that the less he knows, the more the Parisian comes up with lists (that is, peacock syndrome). It is of course untrue, and please excuse the Parisian for knowing that "philosophy is crucial, when you look at authors like Plato, Kant, or Schopenhauer. I mean, you really get things."

As the Parisian's generosity and culture are endless, he will frequently share with professionals his own knowledge of their specialty. So at a restaurant, the Parisian will frequently explain to the chef how to make the best cassoulet: "I usually go with white beans, garlic, sausage. . . ." He will of course always kindly let the taxi driver know the best shortcuts through the city. And he will usually tell the florist the meaning of a bouquet of white roses. Foreigners believe that Parisians enjoy conversing for the sake of it. That is a tragic mistake. Conversations in Paris are a means to act truly generously. A way to enrich others with firsthand knowledge and lists.

Parisians are just a bit more generous than you. Deal with it.

The most skilled Parisians take the list habit to the world of adjectives. They believe in the power of the Parisian tertiary rhythm. The Parisian tertiary rhythm could be described as a list of adjectives. For instance, a play is not just moving. In Paris, a play is "touching, moving, shaking. . . ." A view is not just beautiful. In Paris, a view is "splendid, breathtaking, stunning. . . ." To achieve full Parisian tertiary rhythm, two rules ought to be applied. Never use "and" before your last adjective. And always finish up the list looking somewhat sad and disturbed. Parisians will greatly admire people that master the Parisian tertiary rhythm. To show that he is not taking himself seriously, the Parisian will mock the Parisian tertiary rhythm by turning it into a quintuple rhythm. This is the Parisian's surest chance to seem educated, sensitive, and humorous all at once.

Needless to say, questioning the pertinence of a list is awfully rude. In France, pupils are not to question teachers. Similarly, people are not to question Parisians.

Especially on their lists.

USEFUL TIP: Make sure you always have a notebook when spending time with a Parisian.

SOUND LIKE A PARISIAN: *L'Italie, c'est trop beau . . . Naples, Florence, Rome. . . .*

100%
PARISIEN
APPROUVÉ

Le Ski

For Parisians, *le ski* is not a sport. It is a destination. Parisians go *au ski.*

Parisians usually go *au ski* once a year, for a week. The French Alps is the destination of choice. The Pyrenees are a no-go for they are not only far but also the preferred spot of people from southern France. Therefore lacking elegance.

Picking your Alpine resort makes a strong statement about who you are. Proper resort frequentation is imperative to be accepted in adequate circles. Tignes will bring you respect among real ski fans. Courchevel will gain you acceptance in snob gatherings. Les Ménuires will classify you as struggling.

The primary goal of the annual week *au ski* is to develop the best facial tan lines. Facial tan lines are a strong yet modest statement that, yes, you went skiing and that, yes, the weather was splendid, thank you. For that matter, the odds of finding Parisians on the slopes are low compared to those of spotting some sunbathing on the terraces of the *restaurants d'altitude* sipping on some *vin chaud.* First things first. Parisians know how to stick to their primary objectives. Whatever it takes.

Of course, it is necessary for Parisians to complain about these stupid tan lines on their faces when they come back to Paris. For Parisians are real athletes, they will always have a word about the quality of the snow. Which is always either *excellente* or *dégueulasse.* Anything in between does not exist.

If one year, the Parisian happens not to be able to make it to *le ski,* it is imperative to justify it to other Parisians. Only two reasons will be tolerated: "I was too busy with work" and "I went *au soleil*" (sun, like ski, is a destination for Parisians). Not going *au ski* for a Parisian is like not going to church for a Christian. It jeopardizes your respectability. *Le ski* is part of your identity as a Parisian. No ski, no Parisianity.

For that reason, it is crucial to come back from *le ski* with good stories: you need to be annoyed for meeting so many people you didn't want to meet on the slopes; you also need to tell the story of how you almost broke your arm when this Englishwoman ran into you (she didn't know what she was doing). Your most popular story will be how everyone on the train ride back home was looking at you funny because your luggage smelled a bit funky. Parisians will always arrange to bring back some cheese (Beaufort, Tomme de Savoie, or Reblochon) or *charcurterie* from *le ski.*

Parisians are so bold. You can tell from their stories.

USEFUL TIP: To look Parisian, wear jeans and a sweater on the slopes.

SOUND LIKE A PARISIAN: *Ouais, on a eu de la chance, la neige était excellente.* ("Yeah, we got lucky, the snow was excellent.")

Not Exercising

Besides the common Parisian judgment according to which, if you work out, you are either gay or stupid, the general perception of sports in Paris is that they are retarded and pointless activities. It is therefore seldom practiced by most Parisians.

Yet most Parisians like to remind their friends they used to play sports when they were young: judo, tennis, soccer, fencing, or basketball for young Parisian boys, dance for girls (usually starting with ballet, moving into "modern jazz" as teenagers, though today, "modern jazz" tends to be supplanted by hip-hop or salsa). Most Parisians were actually quite good at the sport they used to practice.

When foreigners jog in the streets of Paris, Parisians will usually smile at them. Which is a rare but in that case much deserved thing. These smiles come in two forms: the marveled-kid smile (think three-year-old kid getting excited when he sees a dog), or the accomplice-in-provocation smile (think of a tennis player smiling when he sees a guy running around naked in the middle of his game on Wimbledon's Center Court). Seeing someone jog takes the Parisian to poetic levels of excitement. He cannot resist this delightfully provocative and refreshing show.

In Paris, joggers are showmen.

The only Parisians who occasionally exercise (usually though not to the point of breaking a sweat) are the ones who have at some point lived in America. There, they discovered a different reality where people can be both intelligent and in shape. So they run. Usually for twenty minutes a week. Maximum. This category of Parisians only shares this imported habit with friends with similar American-infused behaviors. To clarify that they are neither stupid nor gay, those Parisians tend to display poor skills and to wear gear that testifies immediately to their American experience (UNC sweatshirt, NYU T-shirt, Alfredo's Burritos cap).

It is important to realize that exercising is especially ruled out for Parisian women. Parisian women are not to sweat. And not to wear sneakers (except for trendy ones). Most Parisian women deal with it nicely for they tend to dislike sports.

Rather evidently, the physical consequences of substantial and frequent workout sessions (that is, a healthy figure or large muscles) will have you immediately categorized by Parisians as gay or stupid. Parisians are logical.

And prepared: when attacked for their lack of physical activity, Parisians systematically respond "I walk a lot." Parisians are hard to beat.

USEFUL TIP: If you do exercise, don't let other people see that you do.

SOUND LIKE A PARISIAN: *Je faisais pas mal de tennis quand j'étais petit.* ("I used to play tennis a fair bit when I was younger.")

New York

Asking any Parisian where in the world he'd like to live, you will get the same systematic answer: New York.

It is every Parisian's dream to live in New York.

Parisians like to think of themselves as culturally superior. As all people of culture, they shape their perception of reality on cultural masterpieces: in the case of New York, landmarks such as *Home Alone 2, You've Got Mail, The Devil Wears Prada,* and *Friends.* Parisians want to be a part of this New York reality: they want to meet their friends for coffee at Central Perk.

Many Parisians take the step of actually going to New York. For most of them, it is like opening Pandora's box. New York is as vibrant as Paris is asleep; it's as young as Paris is old, as fast as Paris is slow. They were charmed by the beauty of Paris, now they can't resist New York's sex appeal. Paris is every Parisians' wife. New York is their mistress.

Parisians know how living with your wife gets old.

At this point, many Parisians will feel the urge to proclaim publicly their love of New York. New York gear is very popular, especially among the younger generation of Parisians. The *I Heart NY* T-shirt is a must. Worn properly, it can become the utmost element of chic or cool. Less stylish people will opt for an NYPD T-shirt. FDNY gear is exclusively reserved for the gay community in Paris.

Nothing is more chic than having New Yorker friends. Reaching such a cultural pantheon will give the Parisian an irreversible precedence over his acquaintances who do not share their privilege. It is impossible for a New Yorker to be anything but *super cool.* The Parisian with New Yorker friends will usually advise his French friends on the right neighborhoods and bars to visit when in New York. The phrase *un peu underground* will at that point usually be pronounced, often accompanied with a discreetly satisfied smile.

When talking about New York, the French language seems to boil down to three nouns, three adjectives, and one adverb: *énergie, opportunités, dynamisme* on the one hand, *grand, super, génial* on the other. Throw in some *plein* and you can sustain any Parisian conversation about New York. These shiny triptychs certainly help Parisians display their advanced understanding of local social norms.

Because such are Parisians: into social norms and way beyond clichés.

USEFUL TIP: In Paris, stating that you prefer Paris over New York will make you sound old and boring.

SOUND LIKE A PARISIAN: *New York, c'est vraiment super, y a une énergie . . .* ("New York is really great, I mean, the energy . . .")

Wealthy *Arrondissement* Bashing

It is obvious Parisian knowledge that all people living in the same *arrondissement* ("neighborhood") are one. They all talk the same, dress the same, go out to the same places, and have the same professional occupations. This knowledge allows Parisians to practice wealthy *arrondissement* bashing.

This Parisian activity is based on decades of hands-on sociological analysis and is therefore absolutely acceptable. If, as a non-Parisian, you argue this is rough generalization, you will probably be considered "one of them."

Parisians living in the 6th, 7th, 8th, 16th, and 17th *arrondissements* are all *bourges* (short for "bourgeois"). They all drive Smart cars or BMWs. They all spend their vacation in Cannes or Courchevel. And they all wear Ralph Lauren shirts. Only Parisians living in the 16th can be called *gros bourges.* They are all rich and should therefore be punished. A *gros bourge* is like a *bourge,* but worse. No further explanation is needed. Obviously, it is not possible to befriend a *gros bourge* without immediately becoming one yourself.

Brazil has a saying that you always have sex with people darker than you and marry someone lighter than you. The same goes with *arrondissements* in Paris. While sexual intercourse happens between people from different *arrondissements,*

marriages tend to only happen within your own original group.

At this point, it is crucial to realize that wealthy *arrondissement* bashing happens even among wealthy *arrondissement* people. A wedding between a girl from the 6th (Saint Germain des Prés) and a boy from the 16th will appear as a disgrace in the girl's family (cultural degradation, reign of money, loss of class), while it will be viewed as a threat for the boy's family (patrimonial dilapidation, reign of left-wing ideas, absence of dynamism).

When moving into one of the wealthy *arrondissements* from a nonwealthy *arrondissement* or even (God forbid) from another city, it is important for newbies to have a clear understanding that they will lose friends in the process. Social climbing is not well accepted in Paris. One ought to remain poor. In Paris, it's called being polite.

USEFUL TIP: To look *bourge*, and therefore be accepted by wealthy *arrondissement* people, just pop your collar.

SOUND LIKE A PARISIAN: *Tu vois, le mec . . . hyper seizième!* ("That guy, I mean . . . he's so 16th (*arrondissement*)!")

Complaining

While the French have gained a much-deserved reputation for complaining a lot, Parisians take this art to a higher level. In Paris, enthusiasm is considered a mild form of retardation. If you are happy, you must be stupid. On the other hand, if you complain, you must be smart.

A beautiful Parisian syllogism is at hand here: the person who complains is the person who spotted the problem. The person who spotted the problem is the smart person. Therefore the person who complains is the smart person.

This, of course, has deeply affected the Parisian mind. These days, complaining has become the default mode for most Parisians. Making the Parisian a constantly smart person. On top of being, obviously, a lucid one, gifted with the wisdom of not fooling himself with the idiotic perspective of simple happiness. In Paris, complaining is a great remedy to happiness, and therefore to retardation.

With much talent, Parisians manage to constantly tarnish their reality by always finding something to complain about: the food served, people, their jobs, their bosses, the metro, their neighbors, politicians. . . .

The more systematically the Parisian complains, the higher up he ranks in the Parisian hierarchy of intelligent people. The more creative the subject of the complaint is, the more liked and admired the Parisian will be by his Parisian peers (if there is such a thing).

Complaining about the weather or reality television will merely have you accepted by other Parisians. Complaining about highly praised and broadly admired things in Paris like Woody Allen's movies, picnics on the Champ de Mars, or seating at a terrace will immediately place you somewhere between irresistibly original and delightfully iconoclastic.

Needless to say, the idea of actually doing something about what he's complaining about does not cross the Parisian's mind.

In the end, the rhetoric of complaining in Paris is foolproof:

You're not happy but you're smart.

You're not happy because you're smart.

Gosh, it is good to be a Parisian!

USEFUL TIP: For increased levels of perceived intelligence, be creative in the things or people you complain about.

SOUND LIKE A PARISIAN: *Il fait vraiment trop chaud, c'est insupportable.* ("It is really too hot, it's insufferable.")

The Sun

Parisians are sun-deprived most of the year. When the sun comes out, it implicates a drastic shift in the Parisians' habits and interactions.

On a sunny day, it is imperative for Parisians to stress to their friends and colleagues that indeed the sun is out. As most Parisian conversations will start with a weather comment, a sunny day will set the tone for a joyful interaction. Thus, along with the sun, Parisians discover lightheartedness.

Parisian women are the first ones to act out when the sun appears. Warmer temperatures are what Parisian women have been longing for to display the pieces of clothing they've been shopping for over the previous months. The sun is also an excellent excuse for Parisian women to say, *"J'ai rien à me mettre, il faut absolument que j'aille faire du shopping."* ("I have nothing to wear, I *need* to go shopping.")

Consequently, Parisian men do go out more—mostly to stare at Parisian women wearing shorter pieces of clothing. But under the sun, Parisian men also get more in touch with their sex appeal and turn into mean seduction machines. During the summer months, Parisian males will have a tendency to undo three or four shirt buttons. Sometimes five. A beginner's mistake would be to display a gold chain on his naked chest, which would immediately identify him as a *provinciaux*. Seeing

bits of hairy male chests on the streets of Paris will have most American tourists giggling and saying, "Ew, hairy!" The Parisian man will sense that and will feel good about himself, comforted in his ultimate superiority over other human beings.

Under the sun, Parisians become more sexually attracted to one another, more joyful, and more conversant. All this messes up Parisian social interactions based on distance and coldness. Fortunately, it only lasts for a few months. The sun is also a strong hamper to economic activity in Paris as it is commonly accepted that when the sun comes out, you unilaterally shorten your workday to go sit at a café. Parisian bosses hardly argue, for they secretly abide by the same rules. Short skirts and hairy chests should indeed prevail over work. Such is the summertime Parisian wisdom.

USEFUL TIP: Do not wear sporty sunglasses. This is Paris.

SOUND LIKE A PARISIAN: *T'as vu le soleil?! Il faut absolument en profiter.* ("It's so sunny out! We totally need to go out and enjoy it.")

House Parties

Tourists visiting Paris may be disappointed by the Parisian bar and going-out scene.

The main reason behind this is that young Parisians do not go out as much as youngsters from other cities or countries. They do go out. But to their friends' apartments: the Parisian version of a house party. Young Parisians throw two sorts of house parties: *une soirée posée* and *une grosse soirée.*

La soirée posée is a quiet party. Parisians sit on couches, chairs, or the floor, drinking a bit and munching on *des gateaux apéro.* Discussions vary but usually turn political. The atmosphere gets more electric, two camps are usually defined (a heavenly night for a young Parisian man is to be alone against the rest of the crowd) and girls usually end up in the kitchen talking about work, secret affairs, or clothing while guys keep going political. *La soirée posée* is usually improvised the same day and repeated every Friday or Saturday.

La grosse soirée involves more Parisians. More alcohol. More planning. And people dancing. The Parisian is reluctant to throwing a *grosse soirée.* The Parisian usually claims that his place is too small. Which is a bad excuse. Truth is, his place will be trashed by other drunk Parisians. The success of a *grosse soirée* lies in a nice sexual balance and in the diversity of people who attend, ultimately proving not only that the Parisian hosting is generous but also that his friends are really cool.

The predominance of house parties in Parisian culture explains the overall lameness and high foreigner attendance proportion of most Parisian bars and clubs.

USEFUL TIP: Don't bring wine to a *grosse soirée*—that would really be cheap of you.

SOUND LIKE A PARISIAN: *Si tu veux passer à la maison ce soir, j'ai invité deux ou trois personnes.* ("If you want to stop by the house tonight, I invited two or three people.")

Last-Minute Flaking

Foreigners interacting with Parisians complain about their tendency to flake at the last minute. As with every rule in France, the appointment rule is meant to be adapted—humanized, the French would say. Though the reason for flaking can be quite good, it does not matter as much as the time and the manner it is delivered in: common Parisian wisdom is that the later you flake, the more acceptable your excuse is.

Even better, the more unlikely your excuse is, the more credible it will be (the "I'm so so so sorry. You're never going to believe this . . ." strategy). Ultimately, you really need to convince your Parisian friend that you honestly thought you were going to make it until two minutes ago, when this catastrophe happened in your life.

For Parisians who are not daring enough to go for the big lies, three main types of excuses are usually brought to the table:

Excuse 1: "I'm sorry, I'm just too busy. I'm gonna have to cancel."

Excuse 2: "You know what, I'm just exhausted. I prefer to cancel." (Probably the most Machiavellian one as it makes the flaker look like the good guy.)

Excuse 3 is hard to formulate as it is usually hidden

behind excuse 1 or excuse 2. Excuse 3 is that something better just came up. It is the most frequent cause of last-minute flaking.

Parisians do not get angry or upset for last-minute flaking. Usually, they are somewhat relieved because they too probably had something better to do (for example, seeing another friend at the same exact moment on the other side of town). Parisians consider last-minute flaking as advanced time and relationship optimization. Last-minute flaking is therefore broadly practiced and accepted: it is an internalized part of social interactions for most Parisians.

It would be rude to be angry at your friend for flaking on you. All the more so because a real Parisian would have been about to flake on him and his call was actually a relief. If he flaked on you with a mere text message, just give it the usual three weeks of Parisian silence and the incident will be forgotten about. Flaking is no big deal in Paris. Yet it would be unwise to flake repetitively on the same Parisian, especially if that Parisian is a woman.

While onetime flaking is very acceptable, repetitive flaking will be considered a sign of disrespect and poor education. With onetime flaking, you may make a new friend, with repeated flaking, you risk losing an old one.

USEFUL TIP: To prevent last-minute flaking, send a text three hours before the time of meeting to say you're so looking forward to seeing the person.

SOUND LIKE A PARISIAN: *Je suis DE-SO-LE mais je vais devoir annuler.* ("I'm *so sorry* but I have to cancel.")

Urinating in the Street

Urinating in the street has always been a Parisian habit. Visitors may think only bums indulge in street urination. Truth is, most Parisian men have at some point indulged in some outdoor peeing.

Street urinating is mostly a nighttime activity, usually while at a bar or after leaving a bar. It is for Parisian men a group activity and a real moment of friendship. Most groups are made up of two or three Parisian men, sometimes joined by a tourist wanting to live a true Parisian experience. Being asked to be a urinating partner is a very Parisian sort of election that one should appreciate.

Nighttime urinating usually takes place on a little corner or under a porch. Frequently, when about to street urinate with a person they've never street urinated with before, Parisians will first head to the restroom, vaguely see a couple people in there, and say, "This is too crowded. Let's just piss outside." There is no saying no to such an offer. This is a defining moment for any Parisian friendship.

Some foreign men mistakenly believe they have Parisian friends. There is no such a thing as a friendship in Paris that has not been sealed with urine on the street.

While doing your thing, it is important to look cool and detached. A usual and always appropriate conversation is to talk about girls inside the bar. Talking about the boobs of the girl in red is always a safe bet, too. To thank a friend who invited you to urinate outside, you may gently flatter him by telling him that the girl in red, the one with big boobs, really wants him. Consequently, you may be invited outside again later in the evening for a follow-up brief on the girl in red and a detailed action plan for how to proceed.

The *mise en scène* of nighttime street urinating is simple: the Parisian will open his legs quite wide when urinating while at the same time look over his shoulder to see if the police might bust his naughty little Parisian butt. If police indeed catch you, you are most likely to get a warning. For most Parisian police officers are men after all.

Needless to say, urinating on the street is not acceptable for Parisian women. If your female companion finds out you have been urinating in the street, she will most likely call you *dégueulasse*, but deep inside she will start loving the Parisian beast in you.

USEFUL TIP: Impress your friend while urinating in the street by reminding him that urinating in the street is called *délit de miction.*

SOUND LIKE A PARISIAN: *Putain, viens, il faut que j'aille pisser.* ("*Putain*, come out, I have to go take a leak.")

Riding a Bicycle

Parisians like to make a difference. In Paris, that means riding a bicycle. Riding a bicycle is green. And green is good. Good for the environment and good for you. Some ill-intentioned right-wing people will argue that physical effort in the midst of traffic is not physically recommended but they are party poopers.

Besides its obvious greenness, bicycle riding offers clear advantages over riding in a car: bicycles in Paris are quicker and easier to park than cars. Yet, before jumping on a bicycle to save time and the environment, one may want to be notified that in Paris, riding a bicycle carries high political implications.

While pedestrians tend to look at cyclists with a certain affection, a real political war is waged between cyclists and car drivers. They only interact through insults and arm or finger actions. Not only because they endanger each other's lives but more realistically because each judges the other politically.

In the eyes of motorists, cyclists are left wing, dangerous, and unemployed punks. While cyclists think motorists are self-centered, polluting, and vulgar right-wing individualists. Such a war comes to a pause each weekend, when motorists decide to ride their bicycles with their family; soon enough, though, the weekend cyclist will insult motorists for being self-centered, polluting, and vulgar right-wing individualists.

There is a clear hierarchy among Parisian bicycle riders. Riding a mountain bike is pitiful (do you think this is a sport?). Riding a Vélib' is OK (yet uncomfortable). Riding a *vélo hollandais* takes you to the pantheon of Parisian bicycle riding.

La Parisienne, when riding a *vélo hollandais* will immediately gain the favor of all surrounding males. All Parisian men want to fall in love with a girl riding a bicycle.

USEFUL TIP: You need a chip in your credit card to use the Vélib'. Ride with a Parisian if you don't have one.

SOUND LIKE A PARISIAN: *Je me déplace partout en vélo.* ("I ride my bicycle everywhere.")

Macarons Ladurée

Parisians lack imagination. Baby shower? *Macarons* Ladurée. Birthday party? *Macarons* Ladurée. Thank-you note? *Macarons* Ladurée. Dinner party? *Macarons* Ladurée. Weekend in Normandy? *Macarons* Ladurée.

Le macaron has become a key social lubricant in Paris. While most Parisians have given up on ancestral guilty pleasures (sex, drugs, alcohol), very few will say no to the modern form of socially acceptable vice: *le macaron* Ladurée.

Le macaron is a traditional almond- and sugar-based French patisserie. One may now find *macarons* in most Parisian patisseries. But this not a good enough reason to buy them there. For in Paris, buying a *macaron* is not an act of *gourmandise*: it is an assertion of one's social value.

Not to fall into the "disgusting randomly sugar-eating" category, Parisians will always adjunct Ladurée after *macaron,* and thus upgrade themselves from hopeless sugar eater to sophisticated and well-off person. Buying your *macarons* anywhere other than Ladurée is considered either a subversive act or a clear indication of one's lack of knowledge of Parisian social codes. And therefore ruins the point of buying *macarons,* namely making a social statement.

Most fanatics of *macarons* Ladurée are women. While most Parisian women stay away from sugar with somewhat preoccupying discipline, they constitue the main client base of Ladurée. And Parisian women like to make social statements through their purchases (clothes, travel destinations, florist).

The *macaron* Ladurée clearly serves this purpose. But it also allows Parisian women to treat with ill-repressed brutality their weird relationship to sugar: offering *macarons* Ladurée to friends lets the Parisian woman taste them and therefore look like she doesn't have a problem with sugar (note that her attention will be focused all night long on the moment she can indulge in the *macarons* she brought). On top of this, *le macaron* Ladurée is a perverse weapon for Parisian women. Bringing *macarons* to a party will force other women to have at least one. And therefore to gain weight. So the Parisian woman not only feels better about herself but can rejoice for her friends, who also have to gain weight so she doesn't look like the only fat one at the end of the evening.

Parisian snobbery urges shopping only at the Rue Royale boutique. But a quick fix can be found on the Champs-Elysées (aka depressed corporate lawyer syndrome) or Rue Bonaparte (aka Saint-Germain des Prés guilty wife syndrome). The array of reactions when tasting a *macaron* Ladurée is limited. It is either *trop bon* (youngsters), *hyper bon* (cool wannabe bourgeois), or *délicieux* (cheating wife). Parisian wisdom invites sticking to the simple flavors. The most inventive recipes will frequently only fall under the "interesting" adjective. Which is a hidden disgrace for a *macaron*.

USEFUL TIP: Most patisseries in Paris make absolutely lovely macarons.

SOUND LIKE A PARISIAN: *J'ai un dîner ce soir, il faut absolument que je passe chez Ladurée.* ("I have a dinner tonight—need to stop at Ladurée beforehand.")

Wondering What the Point of Living in Paris Is

Parisians are twisted human beings.

Among other twists, Parisians cannot get enough of helpless self-questioning. A very Parisian form of questioning is technically simple to decipher and therefore easy to reproduce for each Parisian in an awful number of situations: they start with a question about their lives, making sure they make it sound like they actually have absolutely no control over their lives. (For instance, "Why am I going out with them tomorrow night?" or "Why do I stay with this company?")

This first question is always followed by a brutally critical appraisal that justifies the question and makes the Parisian look better or deeper than others. (For instance, "Why am I going out with them tomorrow night? I'm so sick of them." Or "Why am I going out with them tomorrow night? I think I need something else in my life." Or "Why do I stay with this company? I'm underpaid." Or "Why do I stay with this company? I think I'm ready for a career change.")

A typical expression of this habit comes when the Parisian returns from a weekend getaway or a vacation outside Paris: "Why on earth are we living in Paris? This is ridiculous."

Among other critical remarks about his hometown, the Parisian will systematically bitch about the nasty Parisian weather and how the people are so rude. In the meantime, the Parisian will never fail to remind you that in the south, the weather is gorgeous, real estate is cheaper, people are "so friendly" and life is just way easier. Yet very few Parisians will actually leave the city for more than a few days. To explain this phenomenon, some blame the lack of quality jobs in other areas of France, others claim that Parisians are ultimately just French and therefore complaint champions and notably change adverse.

To understand Parisians, it is important to realize that such vacuous interrogations are a necessary part of Parisians' psychological balance. Parisians are in constant need for some helpless interrogation ("Why I am alive?" "Why is grass green?" "Why is it raining?"). Being Parisian is about intellectualizing.

Such questioning should always take the form of a real Parisian interrogation. Namely, why. "How" is not a relevant form of interrogation for Parisians. Asking themselves why gives Parisians a sense of self-satisfaction: Parisians only ask themselves real questions, noble ones. A how question would lean toward vulgarity for it would actually drag Parisians into the real world and possibly into actual changes in their lives or perceptions.

Only real questioning matters to Parisians. To be a real Parisian, you just have to wonder why.

USEFUL TIP: Venture outside Paris. Pure countryside is accessible only twenty miles outside *le périphérique*.

SOUND LIKE A PARISIAN: *C'est fou la différence de qualité de vie.* ("The difference in the quality of life is just crazy.")

Rugby

Rugby confronts all the things Paris prefers to turn its back on. While Paris talks, rugby does. Rugby takes strong bodies; Paris prefers to claim that good minds suffice. Rugby faces danger; Paris says there is no such thing. Rugby celebrates brotherhood; Paris worships the individual.

Playing rugby takes as much humility as power; it requires courage and it requires others. It sharpens the body as much as it sculpts the soul. Fraternity is at the center of the sport; conviviality is its rule, simplicity its motto. There is no playing rugby without having a beer afterward. In rugby, the hard and the painful are always followed by the soft and the friendly. Rugby always finishes in conversations, laughter, and legends. Such is the life of rugby.

While all Parisians like to mock the roughness of rugby and of the people who play it, they know there is more to rugby than its apparent brutality; there is more to these men than the bruises on their faces. There is in that sport a form of distinction and an undeniable poetic dimension. On a rugby field, one must run toward the peril, trusting that his team is right there behind him. Life on a rugby field is more noble. Even for Parisians, it is difficult to look down on more noble.

It is also, at some point, difficult to look down on the obvious sense of brotherhood that reigns in a rugby team. The friendships rugby creates life rarely manages to untie. *Les valeurs du rugby* are values Parisians can only look up to. Even though it is a sport, it is OK to like rugby.

Rugby players like to claim that anybody can play rugby. This is true to some extent. On a pitch, there is indeed room for the big and the little, the smart and the stupid, the quick and the nonchalant. Yet sociologically, rugby is mostly played in the upper-middle class. Rugby mixes and confronts but only among a certain category of people.

Parisiennes sense that, except for their tendency to drink and party in excess, rugby players make for good husbands. Parisian families welcome the rugby culture, knowing that it is one that educates about otherness. *Parisiens* appreciate the charisma and testosterone of people who play rugby.

Rugby is after all a tough sport. Rugby is therefore only played by a small number of people. To tell the world that they, too, share the appreciation of rugby, *Parisiens* wear *des polos de rugby* despite their puny bodies and questionable presence. Manliness is progressing every day in Paris.

USEFUL TIP: If you see a Frenchman wearing a piece of clothing with a pink bow on it, it doesn't mean he's gay: he just likes rugby.

SOUND LIKE A PARISIAN: *Dans le train y avait une bande de rugbymans: très sympas, on a bien rigolé.* ("A bunch of rugby guys were on the train: really friendly, we laughed a lot.")

Small Cars

Most Parisians are not fond of cars. Owning a car in Paris is the cause for much more trouble than ease. Lack of parking spots combined with horrendous traffic have turned cars into an awfully slow and expensive means of transportation in Paris.

A closer look at the vehicles occupying the streets of Paris shows that a vast majority comes from *la banlieue.* The Parisian is almost resigned about this: the central part of the street is simply not his world.

There are nonetheless a few Parisians who own a car. If they do, they will most likely own a small car, considering that *ça suffit largement.* Owning a car in Paris imperatively takes owning or renting a parking spot. The car will leave the parking spot only on a few designated occasions: weekend breaks, Sunday outings, and rides to and from train stations or airports. Parisians have long given up taking their car for any other reason.

Owning a small car and finding himself fine with it makes the Parisian look down on anyone owning a big car. These people will immediately be suspected of either overcompensating or of being a *beauf.* The worst *beauf* in the Parisian's view is the SUV owner. If it were up to the Parisian, SUVs would be illegal (except maybe for the old beat-up one that stays at the family country home—but that's different): *Oh et puis l'autre avec son 4x4, il pollue, c'est dégueulasse.* ("That person with the 4x4, he pollutes and it's disgusting.") Small cars are more than enough: *C'est parfait pour les p'tits trajets et puis c'est quand même plus facile de se garer.* ("It's perfect for little trips, and much easier when parking.") Social status in Paris is not gained or displayed through the car one owns. Instead of this utterly provincial attitude, the Parisian prefers to display attributes like the location of his apartment, the destination of his holidays, the restaurants he frequents, and, possibly, for adopted Parisians, the size of the flat-screen TV and the quality of his sound system. For these subjects of consumption, the Parisian seems surprisingly less preoccupied about what suffices or what pollutes less.

Traditional Parisian households may push the limit and own two cars. In that case, there is simply no discussion: one will be a small car and it will be *la voiture de madame*; one will be a big car and it will be *la voiture de monsieur.* Madame will use her car for all the occasions mentioned above plus for those related to the children. Monsieur will take his car daily to go to work. Monsieur will then come back home grumpy, finding himself facing a Gordian knot: staying late at work or being stuck in traffic. Further conversations at this point will usually include phrases like *ce connard de Delanoë* ("this Delanoë jerk"—Delanoë is the mayor of Paris), *pays de cons* ("country full of retards"), *empêcher les gens de travailler* ("prevent people from working"), and *conneries de gay pride et Paris plage* ("gay pride and Paris beach bullshit").

Traditional Parisian households are rarely left wing.

USEFUL TIP: Very old and beat-up cars are considered very cool in Paris.

SOUND LIKE A PARISIAN: *Je peux emprunter la voiture de ma mère si tu veux. Elle est petite mais ça devrait suffire honnêtement.* ("I can borrow my mother's car if you'd like. It's small, but it makes do.")

The Idea of Moving Overseas

Every Parisian softly fantasizes about living overseas. Yet to fully understand the phenomenon, it is necessary to divide Parisians into two groups: left wing and right wing.

Left-wing Parisians see moving overseas as an experience, *un enrichissement.* Oddly enough, the main destination that comes to his mind is New York. Though they like to dabble with the idea of moving overseas, left-wing Parisians consider that France and Paris offer outstanding quality of life, great health care and education, and good infrastructure, and they see no real reason to turn their lives around.

On the other hand, right-wing Parisians spend most of their free time threatening to move overseas. Right-wing Parisians feel isolated, living in a city and a country they know is only going down. They have little faith in their compatriots and in their government. They know that to make it in life, they only have one option and that is to leave. Living a good life in Paris takes a lot of money.

Unfortunately, having a lot of money in Paris requires being born with it. The French economy is slow, salaries are mediocre, and the tax level is high. A majority of the educated right-wing Parisian yuppies lives or has lived overseas for professional reasons: London is a prime destination; Asia is the new Eldorado. Living overseas, they sure miss some things about Paris (mostly the food), but they do not long to come back to the Parisians' grumpy ways and depressing economy.

Right-wing yuppies grew up listening to their fathers advising them to leave the country. Their fathers mostly complained about oppressive taxation on people who work and the disastrous mentality of the vast majority of slackers living off public money. More recent concerns include potential bankruptcy of the state and obvious problems ahead with the radicalization and violence of Muslim populations.

Right-wing Parisians feel like their government does not have the guts to do what it takes. They witness the degradation of their country (financially, intellectually, and socially) and, all things considered, see no option for them but to flee.

Not all right-wing Parisians move overseas. Having built a life and a family in Paris, for instance, makes it difficult. Those are the ones who will complain about the state of the country and advise those who can to go.

There is no doubt today that the most ambitious, educated, and driven Parisian youngsters are leaving the country. One by one. Absence of serious political reaction seems to give them reason.

Once overseas, they will discover pleasures that were so far unsuspected: good money, exciting economy, challenging environment, being surrounded with driven people, and looking at the future with hope.

Evidently in France, political differences vastly lie in the definition of quality of life.

USEFUL TIP: Those Frenchies invading your country are political refugees. Treat them with care, will you.

SOUND LIKE A PARISIAN: *J'ai trop envie de me casser. J'sais pas, n'importe où: New York ca me tente bien . . .* ("I'm ready to crack. I don't know where really: New York maybe . . .")

Clint Eastwood

Parisians like for things to be circumscribed. They like limits. They like to think that things or people cannot be more than one thing. A businessman can have no creative side, a singer can have no business sense. This is life according to the Parisian.

Some elements of life, though, teach them a different lesson. They like to think what they witness is an exception. Something or someone grandiose.

Clint Eastwood was once a gorgeous young actor. He became an immense star. Then a producer. And a director. While still acting. And reinforcing his legend status. Clint Eastwood, in that he exceeds the Parisian, seems to exceed life. Parisians are certain that having overcome his initial condition to do in life what inspired him is the sign of an extraordinary man. They reckon there is something almost divine about Clint Eastwood's life. Parisians would never look at elements like hard work, perseverance, or connections to explain his career. The things that make other people successful are of no help for Clint Eastwood. He's all talent. He's all blue eyes.

The certainty that Clint Eastwood is not only a legend but also an extraordinary man reassures Parisians on his *fréquentabilité.*

Good-looking men happen. Good-looking and charismatic sometimes. Good-looking, charismatic, and intelligent is very rare. Good-looking, charismatic, intelligent, tough, sensitive, talented, and inspiring doesn't. Clint Eastwood is beyond all other human beings. He has had the gift not to stick to himself. The elegance to reveal himself slowly, to pour gently his essence on the world.

Despite his godlike status, Clint Eastwood is a reassuring figure for most Parisians. In his invincibility, he is time passing by and us not caring. He is man becoming better throughout life. He is eyes remaining blue. He is the soul growing under the thick skin. Parisians worry about their eyes becoming gray and their souls wilting. They fear life is not making them a better person.

Clint Eastwood is a figure of hope. May he never die.

USEFUL TIP: The closing theme of *Gran Torino* is beautiful.

SOUND LIKE A PARISIAN: *Clint Eastwood, c'est trop la classe.* ("Clint Eastwood is so damn cool.")

Le 1er Mai

Le 1er mai (May 1) is la Fête du Travail. In France, that means the day is off for Labor Day. This day is among Parisians' favorite days of the year. The first of May is the beginning of spring. After many months of hibernation, the Parisian feels like he can start to blossom again. This is a perky day, full of promises and idleness.

A French tradition on May 1st is to go buy *un brin de muguet* (beautiful-smelling lily of the valley). Street stalls flourish for one day. The scent of the white flower enchants Paris. Every Parisian home that day will be flourished with the traditional lily. In the morning, Parisians walk the streets with a bit of sun on their skin, a bit of joy in their heart, and the satisfaction of having taken the time for traditions and a flower.

For every Parisian, May 1 brings back a set of memories. Every family has its own little *premier mai* tradition—a special destination, a special activity with friends. . . . The Parisian longs to have this spring tradition somehow continued. He finds in these unwritten ceremonies a way to domesticate life in a tender way that makes years going by charming and comfortable.

May is a month all Parisians love. It is usually a sunny one—which would usually explain Parisians jolliness. But if they long for it with so much anticipation, it is primarily because May is the month of *les ponts*.

There are three bank holidays in France in May: May 1 (Fête du Travail), May 8 (Armistice Day, WWII), and l'Ascension (reminiscence of France's Catholic heritage). A *pont* corresponds to the French employee's skillful way to take days off between a given bank holiday and the preceding or following weekend, thus making for a long weekend without diminishing too brutally their number of days off. Three bank holidays in May means potentially three *ponts.* May 1st for most Parisians is like the bell ringing to announce the beginning of fun time.

In terms of business, May is by no means as fully officially "off" as August is. But close enough. While it is reasonable to expect to work in May outside the *ponts,* it would be considered silly to think that any work could genuinely be done during a *pont.* There is a form of national understanding that May is about nice weekends and the matter is not subject to discussion.

The first of May kicks off *ponts* season and there is absolutely no reason not to be as close to happy as a Parisian can be.

Except if the Parisian did not manage to *faire le pont.* Life sometime is just stupidly unfair.

USEFUL TIP: When planning a trip to Paris in May, look out for *les ponts.*

SOUND LIKE A PARISIAN: *Le 1er mai, on passé la journée chez des amis à Fontainebleau. On fait ça tous les ans, on se rerouve, on fait un grand pique-nique.* ("The first of May we spent at our friend's house in Fontainbleau. We go every year and have a picnic.")

Le TGV

Liking is the beginning of weakness. Parisians are therefore not inclined to pour out on what they like. Yet, since considering someone weak for liking a train sounds like an unlikely possibility, Parisians can happily claim that they like le TGV.

Le TGV is France's high-speed train. In a discussion among Parisians about the great things of France, le TGV usually comes first. All French people are in love with the train. Parisians are no exception. But while the great thing about le TGV for *provinciaux* is that it makes Paris closer, Parisians get to enjoy much more. Looking at the TGV map, Paris seems to be the sun. The lines departing from Paris are the rays of light illuminating a dark place called *la province.* Parisians surf on these rays of light.

There is nothing more expected than a discussion about le TGV. Parisians all agree that *c'est hyper pratique* ("very convenient") and *c'est super rapide* ("very fast"). Conversations usually end with *Non, vraiment, c'est top.* Satisfaction all around. There is only one controversy about le TGV. That is, when it comes to going to Nice, is it faster to fly or take the TGV? No Parisian has a definite answer to that question. The twenty-first century still holds a few breathtaking mysteries.

While some Parisians use the TGV for business trips, most use it for good times. *Vacances* or weekends. Le TGV is the perfect partner in crime for a quick escape somewhere in France. *Strasbourg, c'est deux heures vingt, Marseille, c'est trois heures.* Not only is TGV quick and reliable, it is also a fantastic opportunity for the Parisian to book a first-class ticket. First-class flying is out of reach for the vast majority of Parisians, but first-class train travel is only a few euros more. Larger seats. And a plug for the Parisian's laptop. *C'est top, comme ca, je peux bosser ou regarder un film.* ("It's great, this way I can work or watch a movie.") Small luxuries are what the Parisian longs for.

Though a cloudless love story is straight-up impossible for the Parisian, he will enjoy complaining about the price of sandwiches on board. *C'est un scandale* is a phrase that often resonates at that point. When a TGV is late or canceled, the Parisian will systematically complain about how anyone working for the railway company is *un privilegié.*

The idea that going on frequent weekend getaways to precious and enchanting regions could somehow also make him a *privilegié* has never crossed the Parisian's mind.

Just like his beloved train, the Parisian's brain is too fast for these sorts of considerations.

USEFUL TIP: Seventy-five percent of people taking the TGV have a *carte de réduction*. Get one, too—very much worth it.

SOUND LIKE A PARISIAN: *Allez, ce weekend, on se prend un TGV et on va quelquepart.* ("This weekend, let's take the TGV somewhere.")

Calling People *Fachos*

Worldwide, a fascist is a follower or an admirer of the pre-WWII Italian Fascist regime.

In Paris, a fascist is anyone who disagrees with a Parisian and makes a point.

Parisians love to call other people fascists, or more frequently *fachos. Facho* is a crucial word in Paris. It can be used as a noun *(C'est vraiment un gros facho)* or as an adjective *(Tu sais, le type un peu facho sur les bords).* Being called a *facho* is a long-lasting stain that is impossible to remove. It is the ultimate form of offense in Paris, that of poor reasoning in service of disastrous ideas.

Facho, in the Parisian mind, is a term that can characterize a vast array of people. The rarest use of the word *facho* is to define extreme right-wing people. More common use of the word is to be found in situations when someone expresses beliefs and thoughts that are unacceptable to Parisians. The more brutally true the statement is, the more *facho* the person who says it is.

Being a *facho* is about making a point and presenting it without sufficient layers of doubts and qualifications.

Calling someone a *facho* is a fantastic way for Parisians to win a conversation. When a Parisian's dabbling is countered by superior, non-PC, implacable reasoning, the opponent will be called a *facho.* To seal the victory, the Parisian will say, *"On peut pas discuter avec toi"* ("One can't even discuss this with you") or *"C'est dingue de dire des trucs comme ca"* ("I can't believe you're saying things like that"). And walk away. Victory. When calling someone a *facho* is too obviously excessive, the Parisian will prefer terms like *poujadiste* (in the case of a person making a pro–small business statement) or *populiste* (in the case of a politician making a statement most people agree with). *Poujadisme* and *populisme* are the roots of Fascism to the Parisian. They will be fiercely fought against. Do not support small businesses—that would make you a fascist.

In Paris, it is broadly accepted that some groups of people are *fachos.* All extreme right-wing activists, extreme left-wing activists, people in the military, and traditional Catholic families who spend their vacations in Brittany are *fachos.* No exception to this rule exists. Furthermore, all people who, at some point in their lives, have associated in a conversation related to origin, race, or religion are *fachos.*

No matter how relevant the argument is, in Paris, you do not want to be called a *facho.* Ironically enough, the thought that calling people *fachos* is the newest form of mental and moral police does not cross *fachos* callers' minds. *Facho* callers are here to fight the threatening risk of one day seeing Fascism rule Paris.

With enemies like this, Fascism certainly does not need friends in Paris.

USEFUL TIP: Only use the word *fasciste* in political discussions. In normal conversations, *facho* is more relevant and usually sufficient to pour discredit over your fellow converser.

SOUND LIKE A PARISIAN: *Ouais, mais Sarko c'est un facho. . . .* ("Yeah, but Sarkozy is a fascist. . . .")

Going to the Movies on Sunday

The question "What is your least favorite day of the week?" only has one answer in Paris. That is Sunday. The dreaded *dimanche.*

While Sundays have the same flavor everywhere in the Western world, Parisians dread it more than any other Westerner. While other Westerners might dislike the bittersweet feeling of a weekend ending and a new workweek starting, Parisians just loathe Sundays. Parisian Sundays are not bittersweet.

They are bitterbitter.

Weekends for Parisians are not strictly moments of rest. They are implicit social challenges. Each weekend, Parisians need to accomplish things worth sharing with their friends or colleagues on Monday. Weekend descriptions always start out with energetic Friday nights, Saturdays, and Saturday nights. Weekend descriptions at that point get thrilling: the Parisian can display his interests, purchasing power, or connections. The Monday morning coffee break is thus a fascinating social rundown. But the description stalls when Sunday is to be reported. *Et dimanche, pas grand chose, tranquillou, repos.* Plain Parisian lie: depressing boredom travestied as pleasant rest.

In more truthful conversations, Parisians happily agree that *le dimanche, c'est horrible, c'est complètement mort, tout est fermé.* Indeed. So *dimanches* in Paris come in three forms: all day at home doing nothing; all day at home doing nothing except for lunch with the family or brunch with friends; or either option sprinkled with a movie at some point during the day. People going shopping in le Marais on Sundays may well live in Paris but cannot be considered Parisians. Part of the Parisian identity is knowing that *le dimanche* is a lost day and not having any form of hope about it. If you have hopes for your Sunday, you're a newbie or a tourist.

Parisians know that if reality is gray, a movie theater is a good place to try to reset its color for a while. Pitch black. Colors. Emotions. And the hope to keep sliding down that sweet toboggan for the rest of your Sunday. Paris is the city in the world with the greatest number of cinemas. Yet they are all obscenely busy on Sundays. Parisians—discreetly—remain romantics. Hopeless but romantics.

Because Sunday is a day of minimal social efforts, the film will not usually be followed by a drink. Friends who share a movie on Sunday have reached a form of friendship that does not weigh itself down with unneeded exchanges. There is in this Sunday-movie company an unspoken declaration of friendship: "Yes, my Sunday sucks but I'm happy to show that to you." No masks needed. No extra conversations needed—the line was long enough. *Demain sera un autre jour.* This Sunday movie has a Sunday taste.

It is easy at that point to spot a good movie: one that softly managed to turn gray day into sun day.

USEFUL TIP: Save your Parisian Sunday: come to Ô Chateau for some food, some wine, and some fun.

SOUND LIKE A PARISIAN: *Tiens, dimanche, j'ai vu un film pas mal. . . .* ("Sunday I saw a pretty good movie. . . .")

Considering Mental Affliction a Sign of Intellectual Superiority

Parisians value intelligence more than happiness. In Paris, happiness is the sad symptom of an atrophied brain, the curse of the stupid, the limbo of the ungifted.

Mechanically he who is not happy is gifted, he whose brain does not agree with the world is intelligent. The more brutally unfitting the person is, the more gloriously superior his brain is. In this undeniable logic lies the utter privilege of the crazies: that of being looked up to by the Parisian.

The inability to handle the vicissitudes of life testifies to the Parisian's acute perception of the incertitudes and difficulties that make up life. Knowing that life is about incertitudes and difficulties is pure intelligence to the Parisian. Therefore, if they were to choose between being an irremediably unhappy creative genius or a perfectly happy nobody, most Parisians would opt for the grandiose life of misery. If misery is the price to pay for intelligence, Parisians are happy to open wide their wallets.

The glory points of the craziness package do not come distributed evenly. Some afflictions score higher points than others. Schizophrenia, for instance, inspires much less admiration than beautiful depression. When afflicting upper-class people, some mental conditions stemming from or resulting in self-destruction become psychological pantheons. For instance, alcoholism.

The affliction Parisians look up to the most is insomnia. Parisians all wish they could claim for their bed to be crossed by the unstoppable train of the unresting thought. Parisians admire insomniacs for whom they truly are: people devoured by the discomfort of thinking. Insomnia is the most elegant claim of the active brain. All Parisians wish they could be the victims of their fully ruling brain. Slaves to a cerebral monarchy. The fact that being an insomniac is pure torture is irrelevant.

Longing to be something or someone in Paris by no means relates to pursuing these desires in reality. What Parisians cannot get enough of is poetic aspirations. As much as they love them, they are happy with a quite prosaic life.

Crazy is a lovely thought in the end. Crazy to the Parisian is the living evidence that being a tad more intelligent than he is equals craziness and misery. Really, the Parisian got lucky. Intelligent. But not crazy.

That was close.

USEFUL TIP: If you are in Paris and suffer from a mental affliction, start wearing unusual clothes and call yourself an artist. Maybe that's your path.

SOUND LIKE A PARISIAN: *Ouais, ça va. J'ai un peu de mal à dormir en ce moment, mais ça va. . . .* ("Yeah, I'm OK. I am having problems sleeping at the moment, but I'm fine, yeah. . . .")

Bitching About Waiters

When it comes to service, Parisians all wished they lived in America. They all long for torrents of smiles, deluges of friendliness, and avalanches of first names. But reality is stubborn.

They live in Paris.

And Paris is no America.

In France, torrents of smiles, deluges of friendliness, and avalanches of first names do not mean good service. It means you're surrounded with drunken people. And drunk people rarely wait tables. Parisians are quite categorical when it comes to waiters in Paris. They know for a fact that they are all *pas aimables.* Most of them are actually *des gros cons.*

That reality is nonnegotiable. Parisians will never accept that anyone would pay a compliment to Parisian waiters. Bitching about them is one of the rare things that connects Parisians to the rest of the world.

A Parisian never wonders about the cause of what he reckons to be poor service. He will systematically dodge the question by saying, *"C'est pas de ma faute s'il a un job de merde."* Usually adding, *"Y a trois millions de chômeurs. S'il est pas content, qu'il fasse un autre boulot, putain."* ("There are three million people unemployed. If you're not happy, go find yourself another job, *putain.*") Parisians are people of compassion. They will never

put their own rudeness and absence of smiles in question. Neither will he ever include tipping in the beautiful scale of his transatlantic comparisons.

In Paris, clients and waiters don't think much of each other. In an admirable whirlwind of reciprocal passive aggression, tensions add up and poor service usually ensues.

For that matter, when one day, for some peculiar reason, the Parisian or the waiter happens to be in a good mood, the interaction feels like a fresh breeze in the desert, a lightning bolt of conviviality. The waiter will immediately be qualified as *hyper sympa*. The Parisian will enjoy the moment immensely and ultimately pass the address on to all his friends.

The idea to try to be friendlier in order to make happier moments less rare never crosses the Parisian's mind: *C'est pas à moi d'être aimable, putain.*

Clearly, the Parisian is not ready for America.

USEFUL TIP: Parisian waiters like dirty jokes.

SOUND LIKE A PARISIAN: *Il est vraiment pas aimable, c'est dingue.* ("He really isn't friendly, it's crazy.")

Criticizing Parisians

Parisians love Paris. But they hate Parisians.

Most Parisians grow up with a more or less conscious belief in the superiority of Parisians. Because France is an eminently centralized country, Paris concentrates all economic, artistic, and political powers. The brain drain toward Paris is—it seems—brutally at hand. Parisians are the elite of the country. End of the story.

As they grow in age, Parisians get to interact more frequently with people who grew up in different areas of the country and of the world. These encounters end up shedding a new light on their fellow Parisians.

By interacting with *provinciaux* and *étrangers*, Parisians realize these categories of people have the charm Parisians seem to lack of. Pointing out the coldness or rudeness of Parisians is the surest way for Parisians to display to the face of the world their difference and, implicitly, their superiority. When a Parisian criticizes Parisians, he unconsciously crowns himself superiorest among the superiors.

Now, claiming that Parisians are cold, snobby, no fun, close-minded, or rude is not rocket science. The real problem when Parisians criticize Parisians is: then what? The "then what" question is usually not a question Parisians ask themselves. Parisians point at the problem and move on—satisfied with the amount of intelligence they poured on the world.

But when one realizes that the people surrounding him are indeed cold, no fun, and close-minded, he needs to ask himself questions. Even a Parisian.

Once the Parisian realizes that, indeed, Parisians might not be that superior in the end, one major difficulty lies before him. And that is to befriend *provinciaux* or *étrangers.* Parisians usually enjoy these people's freshness and their different approach on life. But befriending someone implies a level of proximity most Parisians just can't or refuse to create with *provinciaux* or *étrangers.* They are happy to have some in their extended network. They will even share good moments with them. But it will be hard for them to connect at a very personal level. Befriending a *provinciaux* or *étranger* for a Parisian is like a guy dating a girl with a big butt.

It is hard to admit socially that this is actually what you prefer.

USEFUL TIP: If you criticize Parisians in front of a Parisian, he will treat your argument with scorn. *Provinciaux* or *étrangers* just don't get it. Only Parisians can criticize Parisians. Only Parisians get it.

SOUND LIKE A PARISIAN: *Non, et puis les gens sont froids à Paris, c'est horrible.* ("And I mean on top of it, people in Paris are so cold, it's horrible.")

Les Petites Vestes

Parisian men have a disloyal relationship to elegance. They cannot cope with it daily. Simply because Parisian men were once Parisian boys. And Parisian boys were meant to dress well. A day of ugly looks is a pleasure that Parisian men like to treat themselves to at least once a week. This is their weekly claim to freedom.

The rest of the week, Parisian men are to maintain a certain level of elegance. Tremendous and shiny Italian-like elegance is not suitable: *m'as-tu-vu.* Nor is stiff and excessively proper English-like elegance: *trop coincé.* Parisian men like for their clothes to be simple, discreet, and elegant. *M'as-tu-pas-vu* somewhat. Their best ally in that daily quest for a nondisputable yet nonsuspectable elegance is *la petite veste* ("suit jacket").

Parisian men love their jackets. A jacket is to the Parisian man what the purse is to the Parisian woman: rather than an accessory, it is a real expression of the mood, social status, and personality of the person who wears it. Fabric, cut, and color depend on season, occasion, and company.

Parisian men—and that is one of the rare characteristics they share with the rest of their gender—can't be bothered with buying clothes regularly. They want reliable pieces of clothing they know will fit and match given social situations. *La petite veste* for that matter is unrivaled.

The jacket is usually taken from a suit. But it can easily be worn with jeans or khakis. With *chaussures de ville*, or sneakers. *La petite veste* must be *bien coupée*. And, because *le Parisien* is quite the sexy man, always *légèrement cintrée*.

The Parisian usually only finds out about *la petite veste* in the second half of his twenties. Before that is simply too soon. As it is, *la petite veste* is the most perfect sartorial transition into the older age. The Parisian's way to start looking like his father while being so obviously cooler than him. "I'm not old, I'm successful and stylish." Best not to remind him at this point that wanting to display success and style is rarely something children like to do.

USEFUL TIP: Two colloquialisms: *retourner sa veste* means "to change sides" and *se prendre une veste* means "getting turned down."

SOUND LIKE A PARISIAN: *Tu mets une p'tite veste, un jean, et puis voilà, tout simple!* ("You wear a sportscoat, jeans, and voilà, simple!")

The Idea of Being a Bon Vivant

The Parisian did not grow up on the fields. As a child, he never explored the world firsthand. He learned through books, school, and television. Experiencing most things by proxy. The logic that shaped him as a child rarely gets overthrown when he grows up.

The Parisian is happy to let others experience life for him. He knows life enough through what he hears from others. He knows the flaws of the paths they follow; he knows the pains and troubles. And he doesn't want any of that.

Le bon vivant sits at the top in the hierarchy of figures the Parisian likes yet would never become. *Le bon vivant* likes to eat, drink, and laugh. With his brilliant knowledge of Ancient Greek philosophy, the Parisian will like to refer to the bon vivant as *un épicurien.*

Yet he's not. His asceticism is to deprive life from lean moments. His generosity is to value nothing more than this very second. The Parisian senses candor where he should see resolution. He perceives simplicity where wisdom truly lies. He sees excess when he should just sit down and have a bite.

Parisians admire the ability some people possess to simply enjoy and have fun. Very few Parisians manage to find a way to that sense of letting go. They need to watch themselves. They do frequently wish it was not so, but it is: they are stuck with themselves.

The sight of the bon vivant is a pleasant one for the Parisian. All at once, he sees joy and he sees food; he sees fun and he feels soothed. He also sees an overweight person and at that very second feels truly wise for not living his life. The gray wisdom of the skinny. Parisians over forty years old at that point will usually think about the heart attack the bon vivant will inevitably have when he turns fifty. All this comforts the Parisian in his lifestyle. It is quite enjoyable.

But the sight of the bon vivant is nothing compared to the thought of it. Brain is more powerful a pleasure instrument than poor eyes could ever be. The thought of a bon vivant is an infinitely comfortable one for the Parisian. The bon vivant is the last Mohican of a France that Parisians wish was not vanishing. A France of good food, full glasses, and jolly people. This France is dying and Parisians know it too well.

Putting yourself on the line is not a Parisian thing to do. If there is a war to wage, the Parisian will fight it talking. Not protesting. Or resisting. And certainly not eating and drinking in what he reckons to be excess. *Le bon vivant* is not a *resistant.* But the Parisian wants to support him. He wants to be on what he senses to be the right side. That of the good guys. That of a better life.

As he does, a few days later, the Parisian will undoubtedly start wondering if he has actually gained weight. This is the start of a whole new form of resistance.

USEFUL TIP: Want to meet bon vivants? Try l'Auberge Pyrénées Cévennes in the 11th *arrondissement*.

SOUND LIKE A PARISIAN: *J'étais dans le sud ouest: ils sont bons vivants les mecs . . . foie gras, pinard. Putain, qu'est ce qu'ils picolent. C'est fou.* ("I was in the southwest; those guys are real bon vivants . . . they eat foie gras, drink wine. Gosh, they drink so much though. It's nuts.")

Barbecues

Life in Paris makes barbecuing impossible.

Yet all Parisians love barbecues. For *un barbecue* is first and foremost an event—a rare one for the Parisian. No invitation in the world sounds more appealing to the Parisian than one to *un p'tit barbec.* In the Parisian mythology, *le p'tit barbec* is good news all around: it means sunshine, outdoors, and a cute garden. Being invited to *un barbecue* is a fantastically appealing perspective to the Parisian. Such precious invitations are too rare.

In a Parisian existence, opportunities for barbecues are seldom. The most common one requires a sunny weekend. Usually in early spring or early summer. The scene unfolds at a friend's house in the suburbs or in the countryside, never farther than an hour away from Paris. At this type of barbecue, *rosé* will generally be the drink of predilection. Conversations about holiday plans and how beautiful the weather is will abound. The Parisian has the uncertain but resolute feeling that barbecued meat is healthy. These barbecues will be remembered for years. They can be considered a peek into Parisian happiness.

The second most common opportunity for barbecues is less memorable, but usually just as pleasant. The scene now unfolds at a country house. The Parisian went shopping for what he reckons to be the freshest food in the universe. Incidentally, just a few hours ago—the Parisian has no doubt about it—the fish was still in the ocean, the steak was quietly grazing in the field next door, and the apples were falling off a beautiful tree in some nearby farmer's backyard. *On s'le fait au barbec?!* The most just of all tributes to the freshest of foods.

Parisian men love to *s'occuper du barbec.* In these very minutes where they bring a cautious urban eye to an ancestral gesture, they manage to reconnect with their masculine identity. They feel like, for a few minutes, lighting a fire and grilling steaks, they can act as real men, enjoy it, and be appreciated by others for it.

Finally, barbecues allow Parisian men to be real men and not shameful about it. Realizing that, one may indeed regret that life in Paris does make barbecuing impossible.

USEFUL TIP: Good meat in Paris can be found at Hugo Desnoyer's *boucherie* in the 14th.

SOUND LIKE A PARISIAN: *Samedi, on était invités à un p'tit barbec, hyper sympa, il a fait super beau.* ("Saturday, we were invited to a little barbecue. It was really nice; it was beautiful out, too.")

Lunch Menus

Dinner is the festive Parisian meal. Lunch for most Parisians is merely a utilitarian meal. One should restore in the midst of the workday and that moment is called lunch.

As a student, the Parisian has no money. So lunch for him consists mostly of fast food and sandwiches. As he grows older and starts earning more money, his French genes start tickling him and—though he usually has little time for lunch—he intends to turn it into a satisfying moment. Living in France, all odds are that, no matter how old he is, he still is far from rich. So value for his money is something he will be looking for.

A happy medium is therefore what the Parisian hopes for. Enough ambition of differentiation to clearly separate his taste buds and wallet from that of the plebes. But certainly not enough to even consider going à la carte on anything but the company's card. On his dime, the Parisian goes for *le menu du midi.* A simplified declension of the evening menu offered for something between 10 and 20 euros (U.S.$15–$20). This menu is usually made up of *entrée et plat* or *plat et dessert.* The double-barreled temptation usually turns into a triple-barreled one: supplement for *entrée, plat, et dessert* is usually on offer—most likely, the Parisian reckons, to trouble his peace of mind.

The drink question is an easy one. To the question *Qu'est ce qu'on boit?* that waiters like to ask, Parisians usually respond with a pitiful *une carafe d'eau.* Elusive moment of self-humiliation. At that second, the Parisian feels cheap for not ordering mineral water. And bad for not ordering any wine. He is turning his back on the essence of his country and he knows it. But utilitarianism is never far. Neither are the fearful ways of Parisians when it comes to wine. If one bold Parisian feels like wine, another one around the table will usually calm him down with a wise *"Non, moi, vraiment, j'peux pas, j'ai du boulot cette après-midi."* The voice of reason rarely loses in Paris.

At the end of the meal, the Parisian loves to pop his *carnet de tickets restaurants.* Monopoly money given by his employer to subsidize his lunch expenses. His daily *ticket restaurant* rarely covers the full amount of the lunch menu. Thus, at this stage, he washes off earlier self-inflicted humiliation by contemplating the ego-boosting decision of either pitching in a second *ticket restaurant* or pitching in with a few coins from his own pocket.

Who said meals in Paris were not always delicious?

USEFUL TIP: Best value lunch menu in Paris can be found at le Reminet in the 5th. Dinner there is also eminently enjoyable.

SOUND LIKE A PARISIAN: *Alors on va prendre trois formules entrée-plat. Avec trois chèvres-chauds, deux saumons, et un onglet saignant.* ("OK, we're gonna get three menus. With three warm goat cheese, two salmons, and one hanger steak.")

Reading the Titles of the Books Displayed in a Home They're Invited into for the First Time

Parisians need to be reassured. They cannot accept into their lives people they have little knowledge about. They need to have access to certain crucial pieces of information to decide whether or not the person in front of them is one of quality. They know too well how misleading physical appearance and attire can be. Parisians need to know about achievements. They need a track record to decide whether or not they wish to engage.

Yes, Parisians are that spontaneous.

Propriety in some situations prevents them from accessing the information they need. That is when Parisians turn into full-on bloodhounds. If one lets a Parisian he does not know (or, more precisely, who doesn't know him) into his home, he should be warned that the Parisian will analyze any visible element he can find. While most people will stick to interior design, the Parisian will engage in a discreet but unstoppable review of all the books showcased in the place. While other guests childishly enjoy themselves over a drink and pleasant conversation, the Parisian is on a mission. Walking at a disturbingly slow pace in front of bookcases. Occasionally grabbing one, flipping a few pages, then nodding intelligently while placing the book back on the shelf.

The Parisian will thus grow tremendously informed about his host. He will know about his interests—which, if of greater culture than his, will immediately be deemed as solely proclaimed ones. He will most likely find out about his political beliefs and tastes in entertainment. All this is much more precious than drinks and fun conversations.

One thing that will disturb the Parisian is a home where books are plentiful, apparently read recently, and not placed there just as a declarative statement of cultural identity. The Parisian will sense his cultural inferiority and come back to the group ready, if need be, to make his host look like a stuck-up nerd.

Reading the titles of the books never makes Parisians question their own absence or mere lack of reading. The Parisian absorbs all these books and authors as if he knows them inside and out. It is a very comforting thought. Unlike that of the other guests in the room, the company of great minds is one

Parisians can appreciate at once. Great minds have the good taste of having an immediately identifiable track record.

Finally, the Parisian has found someone as polite as him. He can go ahead and mingle now.

USEFUL TIP: Prepare.

SOUND LIKE A PARISIAN: *Attends, sérieux, c'est bon quoi. Le mec c'est Marc Lévy, Paolo Coelho et compagnie, ça va quoi.* ("I mean, seriously. The guy is into Marc Lévy, Paolo Coelho, and stuff. Puh-lease.")

Thailand

In the summertime, there are more Parisians in Thailand than in Paris. Thailand has grown to become Parisians' destination of choice. Since they spend most of their time pondering what is to them the most decisive question of all—where their next holiday destination will be—Parisians look for a destination that has it all.

That destination, to them, is called Thailand. When asked why, they will systematically answer with an irrefutable: *"Attends, c'est hyper beau, y a des temples, de la plage, un peu de culture, la bouffe est bonne et ca ca coûte rien: tu peux te mettre des hotels incroyables."* ("Listen, it's gorgeous, there are temples, beaches, a bit of culture, the food is good, and it costs nothing: you can get an incredible hotel.") Super combo. There is no beating that.

Parisians who have been to Thailand long to go back. Parisians who haven't will soon enough. A man needs to rest. And Thailand is perfect for that. *Tu peux te faire des temples pendant deux trois jours, et après, tu te poses cinq jours dans un hotel de grand luxe, plages de sable blanc. . . .* ("You can do the temple thing for three days, and after that, five days at a luxurious hotel, white sand beaches. . . .") Visiting temples seems like an exhausting thing to do for the Parisian.

Among a group of Parisians, not wanting to go to Thailand makes you what in America would be designated as socially awkward—unless you are over sixty years old, which is a relevant excuse. It seems suspicious to the Parisian that someone would not judge as eminently pleasurable indulging in Thailand's super combo.

Like many Western travelers, the Parisian no longer visits countries. He does them. Checks them off his list. In Paris, that list is the longest one in the world. Parisians have a lot of time off and on average have more money than other French people. As it is long, that list also gets deep. While Thailand sits at the top of the hierarchy along with destinations like Bali, one will find, in the unfathomable darkness of the bottom of the list, destinations like the Dominican Republic or Spain.

The Parisian is as deeply saddened by the plague of mass tourism gone rampant as he is by climate change. These legitimate worries get conveniently washed off by the magical hands of those Thai massage ladies.

Really, there is no beating Thailand.

USEFUL TIP: The various Thai islands do not all come with the same glow. Do your homework.

SOUND LIKE A PARISIAN: *A Noël cette année, on va aller en Thaïlande. Un peu de soleil, ça va nous faire du bien. J'en ai vraiment besoin en ce moment.* ("At Christmastime this year, we're going to Thailand. A bit of sun will do us good. I really need it right now.")

Le Burger

Some people think Parisians are Parisian. Wrong. Parisians are New Yorkers. As such, they love a good burger.

Burgers were once looked down upon in Paris: *On n'est pas des Americains, bordel.* Imperialism had its limits and the doors of a French restaurant were definitely one. Hamburgers were to food what Jerry Springer was to television. Something Parisians were not ready to cope with. Something America could keep to itself. But things have changed.

As Parisians started becoming New Yorkers, what was uncool about America started no longer being despised but simply made fun of, while what was cool about America started no longer being ignored but instead adopted.

A good burger is undoubtedly one of the cool things about America. Over the past decade, burgers started flourishing on the menu of many Paris *bistrots* and restaurants. A key criterion to place a Paris restaurant on the hipness scale is the number of dishes you could find at a New York restaurant. Have a hamburger, a Caesar salad, and a BLT on your menu and your restaurant will officially be hip.

Optimists would expect the French to make the burger even better. But optimists certainly do not hang out at hip Paris restaurants. Most burgers there are quite forgettable. The best part about a Paris hamburger is its price. It is virtually impossible to find a burger in Paris for less than 13 euros (approximately U.S.$16). Even gastronomic restaurants have started offering a gastro-burger, usually with foie gras in it.

When ordering a burger, the Parisian needs to show how much of a New Yorker he is, how comfortable he can be with the whole burger thing. So he will rarely order *un hamburger*. Most likely, he will ask for *le burger* or, in the case of a cheeseburger, for *le cheese*. The nickname *"burgie"* recently came up among younger Parisian men.

It is indeed an absolute fact that no Parisian woman has ever ordered a burger at a restaurant. Ever.

Lovers of timeless Paris can—after all—rest assured.

USEFUL TIP: Burgers do not come with coleslaw in Paris—for good coleslaw, go to a *traiteur*.

SOUND LIKE A PARISIAN: *J'me ferais bien un p'tit burgie.* ("I'd like a little burger right now.")

Cobblestone

Parisians dislike the idea of concrete. Concrete sounds urban and gray. They are no fans of the idea of asphalt either.

They do, on the other hand, love cobblestones. They love every single thing about them. Cobblestones are one of those rare things each and every Parisian finds fully likable. Full-on unanimity.

This unanimity finds its roots in the mystique of cobblestones in France. Cobblestone is medieval France, festive, and yet-to-become-glorious France. On these stones, carriages of all sorts have carried goods, ideas, and people. Cobblestones are part of the decor of France. Cobblestones feel like home to the Parisian.

The history of cobblestones was rather uneventful up until May 1968. Massive protests in France, a taste of *petite révolution.* Students and workers together united against the bourgeois society. The key slogan of this striking movement was *"Sous les pavés la plage."* ("Underneath cobblestones is the beach.") Cobblestones suddenly became the symbol of an indulgent revolution. They still showed the way, just a different way. They gained a poetic and libertarian dimension. Roads could also have been undone. Paved in a different way.

The nature of cobblestone roads in Paris reflects this dual identity. Infinitely historic and traditional, while somewhat

poetic and revolutionary. Cobblestone streets are bumpy. At first. Then urban erosion does to rocks what it frequently does to souls. Makes them flat.

The noble mythology of cobblestone in Paris also has to do with a bicycle race: le Paris Roubaix. Every year, pro cyclists leave Paris to cycle to northern France's Roubaix. They have to cross the much dreaded Travée d'Arenberg, a rider's version of hell. Cobblestones and rain.

Cobblestones make life tricky and bumpy. They make it uncertain and poetic. On the streets of Paris, in these cracks between cobblestones resonates a bit of the Parisian soul.

Who said Parisians were not down to earth?

USEFUL TIP: High heels and cobblestones rarely work well together. Keep that in mind for your next after-dinner romantic stroll.

SOUND LIKE A PARISIAN: *Non, un appart top . . . sur cour, tu vois, une petite cour pavée: hyper mignonne!* ("A great apartment . . . the building has a courtyard with cobblestones: super cute!")

Les Planches de Charcut

Parisians are aways torn between dieting and being a good friend. Parisian women have vastly solved the problem by meeting up with their girlfriends over tea (woo-hoo!). Parisian men on the other hand usually give in and opt for food and drinks. In the crack of persisting shadows of Catholic guilt grew the concept of conviviality.

Parisians like the idea of conviviality. There is no conviviality in France without food or drinks on the table. Certain types of food and drinks score more conviviality points than others. In the world of food, nothing is more convivial than *qu' une petite planche.* Literally, *une planche* is a board, a plank. In a Parisian bar or restaurant, there are three types of *planches*: *les planches de charcut, les planches de fromage,* and *les planches de fromage et charcut. La charcut* is short for "charcuterie": an assortment of smoked and cured meats (*saucisson, rillettes,* pâtés, ham) usually served with a few cornichons. *Fromage* is "cheese": that *planche* consists of a selection of cheeses (Camembert, Brie, *Comté, bleu*). A bread basket on the table and . . . *la vie est belle!*

Nothing can accompany a glass of wine before a meal better than *une p'tite planche.* Nonprocessed artisanal products served on a wooden board sure start to sound like genuine stuff. Genuine is the beginning of convivial. A first glass of wine leads to the first *planche,* which leads to the second glass, which itself leads to the second *planche,* and so on. . . .

Ordering a *planche* differentiates the Parisian from a tourist at aperitif time in Paris. The tourist will just go for the wine. So passé. It is key for the Parisian man to keep in mind that a Parisian woman will only pretend to enjoy it. Even though she is a total party pooper, she does not want to come across as one. But as soon as the waiter brings the *planche,* she will long for one thing only: for that *planche* to be empty. Or gone. She will pretend to listen and enjoy the conversation while most of her energy will be solely dedicated to not giving in and not touching this food. If a gentleman insists, she will come up with her favorite line: *Non, merci, j'ai pas trop faim.* This, of course, is an absolute lie. But looking skinny comes at a price. And passing on a good *planche* is definitely a part of it.

More for the boys!

USEFUL TIP: *Planches* are sneaky little things. Watch your back.

SOUND LIKE A PARISIAN: *On s'prend une p'tite planche? Charcut? Fromage? Comme tu veux . . .* ("Let's have a little *planche? Charcuterie?* Cheese? As you like . . .")

Wanting to Start a Business

Being active socially in Paris might be misleading. Meeting up with Parisians for dinner, in bars, or at parties, one may draw some hasty conclusions. One of them could be that the flame of entrepreneurship is consuming every Parisian soul.

Any conversation about professional life in Paris will necessarily have one Parisian say, *"Je réfléchis à monter ma boîte."* ("I'm thinking of starting my own business.") The Parisian indeed does think a lot. He first thinks that he is not fully *épanoui* ("full-blown") in his current job. *L'épanouissement* is a new Parisian objective. Happiness through work. Over the past two decades, work has stopped being an activity only to provide sufficient money to pay for needs and desires. Work started being about learning things, interacting with interesting people, and having fun. Which probably means that leisure time was about completely different things.

So awkwardly enough, most Parisians find themselves not fully *épanouis* in their job. For some reason, they deem that starting a business will put them in a completely different spot. No boss, no hierarchy, no pressure. Unfortunately, some things prevent them from *se lancer*. Starting a business would mean letting go of their salary, their vacation time, their *mutuelle*, their *comité d'entreprise*, and all the other advantages that come with being an employee in France.

The typical entrepreneurship adventure of the Parisian starts in college. They opt for a job with a company for two years (*pour le CV, pour apprendre, pour l'expérience*). After these two years, they'll start their business for sure. Two years later, they did enjoy those three weeks in Thailand last summer, and conveniently, they just got a raise. But the Parisian is still thinking very hard of a concept. Thinking, thinking, thinking . . . Harder than ever. His girlfriend plans a trip to Argentina in the winter. Then comes buying an apartment, getting married, having babies, taking care of the children. The Parisian would love to start a business but *ça ne serait pas sérieux, c'est hyper risqué.* Time flies by and now the Parisian knows he'd be a really good entrepreneur. But he makes enough money and is not ready to let go of his position after all these years. Then comes the endearing shadow of retirement. The Parisian promises to start a business a few months later, mostly to take advantage of his experience and to occupy his days. But traveling continues and madame wants to move somewhere sunny. Not fully compatible with a new professional adventure.

The rare Parisians that one day actually start a business have to go through the discovery of an icy French reality. That of the social scorn related to anything business. Starting a business, one may only drop down the great Parisian social ladder. Either he does not do well and is immediately considered an irremediable loser, or he does well and then starts being considered an astute, money-driven, sneaky person. And of course culture deprived. The corollary of success in business in France is an immediate loss in the view of others of any sense of refinement, culture, and ideals. You do well so you're evil. You do well, probably, actually, because you're evil.

Though the Parisian is not aware of the icy treatment entrepreneurs receive in Paris, one may suspect that he senses it. And that, unconsciously, his desire to start a business has to do with the life-long repressed desire to no longer be a good boy.

USEFUL TIP: Do start a business. Just not in France. France truly is the worst country to make money, but the best one to spend it.

SOUND LIKE A PARISIAN: *Ouais, je sais pas, je réfléchis. Je monterais bien ma boîte, mais j'sais pas, c'est chaud quand même.* ("Yeah, I don't know. I'm thinking about starting my own business. But I don't know, it's tough really.")

Relationships

For visitors, Paris is the City of Love. For Parisians, it is the City of Relationships. Every Parisian is in a relationship. That relationship is more or less official, more or less successful, but it always *is*. Consequently, there is simply no singles scene in Paris. If sexual tension is what makes a city fun, Paris has officially become the most boring city in the world.

All young Parisians are in relationships. For them, the main reason to be in a relationship is not to be single. Most young Parisians are averse to life: they see most things as threats, most risks as primarily dangerous, most singular paths as awfully unsafe. Danger for them is around every corner. They think relationships are round little things with no threatening corners; the threats of a relationship they feel they master and choose—this feeling is a reassuring one. Therefore their relationships are long-lasting ones. Not quite good enough to get married, not quite bad enough to break up.

Being single after the age of twenty-six is the clear indication of a troubled mind. If not a troublemaker, that person has got to be a trouble seeker. While the English language has the good taste of distinguishing "alone" from "lonely," French only offers *seul*. Not being in a relationship means being *seul*. The threatening shadows of loneliness, only darkened by the local inexistence of celibacy.

Most surrounding elements create the perfect scenario for a life of romantic dissatisfaction: absence of a singles scene leads to sticking with the wrong person, which itself leads to many a frustration, which inevitably—in a nonreligious city—leads to divorces and breakups a few years down the road. Older Parisian men who still have a form of moral and religious grounding do nonetheless stick with their spouses (unless it is the other way around). They like to flirt and compliment beautiful women—which usually amuses the French and shocks foreigners. That charming France—sadly—is vanishing.

Courting is no longer a Parisian habit. The only way Parisian men like to play it is safe. Parisian women on the other hand, caught in the double obligation to be neither sluts nor single, become not desirable. Absence of flirtation becomes the norm after the age of twenty-six. Curtains closed.

The dry local environment inhibits natures and ambitions. Ironically enough, as Parisians are more and more in relationships, they become less and less likable. Which, needless to say, makes them stick to their relationships even more.

USEFUL TIP: If you have a vague fantasy about Parisians, rest assured, the few that do not follow the pattern explained above usually end up with foreigners. Those are the wise ones.

SOUND LIKE A PARISIAN: *Ils sont ensemble depuis cinq ans. . . . Ouais, ça se passe bien je crois. . . . Non, ils sont pas mariés, non non.* ("They've been together for five years. . . . Yeah, it's been going well, I think. . . . No, they aren't married.")

UNICEF Cards

Current Parisian culture has a greater inclination to assist than to construct. If he's in a position to give, the Parisian won't try to build something: he will contribute.

In the Parisian scale of generosities, that to children scores the most points. There is no better deed in life than helping a child in need. Unlike other charities, those that help children are therefore never suspected of being vaguely corrupt or paying their staff too much. The Parisian wants all the money to go to the kids—that is, when it comes to donations, his insuperable rule.

UNICEF is a charity Parisians don't know a whole lot about. But, damn, it sounds good. Fully international, global spread, helping children, promoting education . . . and making calendars and cards. Parisians love the idea of the three in one. By buying a UNICEF card, they send greetings to someone that matters to them, they show they care about poverty, and they help kids. UNICEF cards make all other greeting cards look crass.

The cards Parisians will prefer are the ones showing cute faces of dark-skinned children. It is important for these children to smile or look cute. Images of simple joy are something Parisians cannot get enough of. Add cute children, extreme poverty, and the feeling that he has helped and you'll plunge the Parisian into mild bliss. The Parisian will usually leave this card on his desk or on his fridge. For quite some time. He will make a note to himself to start sending UNICEF cards, too.

The Parisian will consider UNICEF cards as an indication of how caring one is—caring, rather than generous. He will have to accept that by sending these cards, he will show a form of Christian heritage. This is not acceptable in all circles: in Paris, it is OK to be religious, but not really a Christian.

No one will ever brag about buying UNICEF cards or calendars. Small treats to one's ego are best left untold—as long as they help children and don't go unnoticed.

USEFUL TIP: Happy New Year cards are sent in January in France. Score extra points by sending a UNICEF card for a different reason, at a different time of year.

SOUND LIKE A PARISIAN: *Oh, t'as vu les p'tits là, trop mignons. Ils sont trop choux les p'tits Indiens. Ou alors ils sont Malgaches? Enfin, trop mimi!* ("Oh, you've seen the little kids, so cute. Indian children are so cute. Or are they from Madagascar? Anyway, so cute!")

Bashing Tourists

The minute a person becomes a tourist, he suddenly loses most of his respectability. Flying into Paris, hardworking people, good family men, brilliant students, and successful businesspeople get beheaded: they become tourists.

In Paris, there is nothing more degrading than being a tourist. Tourists are all the same: they have no clue, no taste, no nothing. Some have money and, in that case, it is all they have. Parisians would never want to befriend a tourist. That would be an absolute humiliation.

Tourists seem to accumulate mistakes, as if their sole ambition during their whole stay in Paris is to annoy Parisians. Tourists wear sneakers, they walk slowly, they're loud and wear dubious colors, they get lost in the metro, they are amazed by every little thing. . . . Tourists are painfully identifiable to the Parisian.

Any activity that has to do with tourists necessarily sounds like a rip-off to the Parisian. The idea that a tourist can be well informed or make sound decisions about how to spend his time or money in Paris is not something Parisians are ready to conceive. In that regard there are only two types of tourists: those who frequent *les pièges à touristes* ("tourist traps") and those who are outrageously rich. The Parisian feels a little bit bad for both. He feels like it is physically impossible for the tourists to get a "real" experience of the city. The idea that some tourists genuinely adore Paris, know it quite well, come back regularly, and know the good restaurants more than he ever will is completely foreign to the Parisian.

Among tourists, Parisians only talk about four nationalities: *les Chinois, les Japonais, les Italiens-ou-les-Espagnols* (*Italie-ou-Espagne* truly being only one country), and *les Américains.* They have precise knowledge about each type. *Les Chinois* travel in groups and they shop at Louis Vuitton. *Les Japonais* are either old, traveling in groups and taking pictures, or young with funny haircuts and outfits. *Les Italiens-ou-les-Espagnols* are just loud. *Les Américains* say "oh my God" and "amazing" every five seconds.

Though these generalities tend to be quite accurate, the Parisian is rarely proven wrong. Which comforts him in the certitude that tourists do not really have souls. They are just there, being tourists, doing whatever it is tourists do. The Parisian despises tourists a bit for thinking that the Paris they see is the real Paris. The real Paris is, of course, his Paris. Tourists' Paris is, in their mind, somewhere between not genuine and too expensive.

While very few of them work directly with tourists, Parisians realize that they have a positive impact on their city's economy. They also get to experience firsthand their impact on the prices of real estate and the subsequent redefinition of the city. One by one, wealthy winners of the new global order kick Parisians out of Paris, turning Paris into a mere beautiful shell. Ironically enough, Paris lovers from around the world, with nothing but good intentions, orchestrate the silent agony of the charm of the city. This awfully modern pattern, fully at hand for instance in the 7th *arrondissement,* pushes simple people to the outskirts of the city. The social melting pot of workers and families that once made Paris is slowly but surely being turned into a global melting pot of the wealthy, contemplating childishly the France they dreamed about and the Parisians they wanted to meet.

In this convenient world, it is not uncommon for tourists sitting in a Parisian restaurant to realize that they live a few blocks away from one another. The Parisian waiter who witnessed the scene will think about this unlikely encounter on his train ride, back to his studio in the *banlieue* . . . thinking with a smile that it's crazy.

Who said Parisian waiters were not nice people?

USEFUL TIP: As a tourist, be nice and smiley to Parisians. It does wonders, you'll see (they're not used to it).

SOUND LIKE A PARISIAN: *Oh, les touristos, putain, j'y crois pas. . . . Tu l'as vu l'autre avec sa banane, ses baskets et son appareil photo: champion du monde!* ("Look at those tourists, *putain*. I can't believe them. . . . You see the one with his fanny pack, sneakers, and camera: he's a world champion!")

Buying the Paper While on Vacation

Parisians would like for life not to change. They would like to be the only ones progressing in a stable world.

Away on vacation, this desire to break for a minute the pace of modernity reaches a new peak. As most urban Westerners, Parisians long for a taste of a world that is still free from the tyranny of information and pressure. Modern treats are soft ones: Parisians will regularly seek destinations where the world as Parisians know it has not caught up yet. The ultimate break is about being reassured that some things, no matter what, do not and will not change.

For that reason, the Parisian cherishes his breaks to the French countryside. There, he loves the quiet simplicity of life, he enjoys the calm of interactions, he finds charm in things that in Paris bother him, he finds pleasure in activities that in Paris would be a chore.

Simplicity at times can be the greatest luxury. Out on a break, the Parisian will like to wake up in the morning, find a nearby bakery, buy bread and croissants and then the newspaper. By doing so, he feels like he's reconnecting with what a man is to do in the morning; he steps out of the oppressive pace. He contemplates things with more distance. He feels refreshed.

At home, the Parisian does not take the time to read the paper. He will certainly get his daily fix of fresh news online at work or in some free paper handed out to him on the metro. But rarely will he actually buy the paper, sit down, and read it quietly. The perception of news away from home is also quite different. So will be its impact. News matters less on vacation. Seeing that, outside of his own, there is a world that does not seem to budge makes him consider the events that in Paris revolt or scandalize him with a form of ephemeral wisdom. Out in the countryside, the Parisian does not let the world affect him as much.

Being outside of what he reckons the world is, he suddenly looks at it the same way the sober one looks at the drunkards at a party. Somewhere between amused, scared, and sad but always somewhat reluctant to join them.

Chez le marchand de journaux, on top of the newspaper of the day (which can be a national one or—for Parisians with a regional rooting—the local one), Parisians like to buy at least a second item: *L'Equipe* for men, and a women's magazine for *la Parisienne.* Later that day, only the men will read *L'Equipe*, while everybody will flip—more or less attentively—the pages of the women's magazine. *La Parisienne* will systematically look for partners *pour faire les tests.*

Away in some country home, the Parisian loves to light a fire. To do so, he will use some old newspapers piled up by the fireplace. He will take a quick glance at what papers said that day and immediately think that all this news loudness really doesn't matter in the end: every day, more articles get written, but truly life does not change.

This constant confusion between life and the world, between his life and the world, forms a philosophical sway from which the Parisian likes to contemplate. The reassuring movements of his mental sway are the best way to comfort him that, even though he changes, even though everything does and will, he will be fine.

USEFUL TIP: Visit the French countryside.

SOUND LIKE A PARISIAN: *Oh, tu as fais le café?! Et puis y'a des croissants? Et le journal? Oh, merci mon amour.* ("Oh, you made coffee, and there are croissants? And the newspaper? Oh, thank you, my love.")

Scarves

Parisians are not known to be warm. It will therefore come as no surprise that they wear scarves.

Scarves are a crucial element of Parisian life. Much like a boring girlfriend in bed, the Parisian is always a bit cold. When he's not, he knows himself enough to suspect that he soon will be. Consequently, rarely will the Parisian ever venture out without his scarf.

The choice of scarf is a determining social qualifier of both style and *classe sociale*. So is the way one chooses to tie his scarf. Parisians know their scarf will characterize them, identify them, position them, rank them, classify them, distinguish them. There can therefore be no messing around when it comes to choosing a scarf.

Men in Paris usually own one scarf. They play it safe, wearing the scarf they received as a gift from a person that could not stand their old scarf. Women, on the other hand, are more cautious, knowing that scarves are crucial to a person's style. Every Parisian woman owns at least three scarves. Width, fabric, colors, and brand escalation generally lead to them owning more than this.

A good way to determine if a Parisian is into fashion or not is to look for color coordination between her scarf and any other piece of clothing she's wearing. If you spot color coordination, that is the clear hint that this person likes to play it safe, applying old recipes, and therefore that she is not into fashion. Parisians with a sense of style will look down on color coordination. *Colors dégradé* is a different sory.

Parisians like the romantic glow that comes with wearing a scarf. Men think of poetry, women of floating elegance. Both would like for their scarf to dance with the tormented winds of Paris. But it won't.

Parisians are no Isadora Duncan and, for some utterly Parisian reason, they somehow regret it.

USEFUL TIP: Even though recommending cashmere does sound very snobby, you must admit it is soft.

SOUND LIKE A PARISIAN: *Une idée cadeau? Je sais pas, une écharpe?! Il porte des écharpes?! Bon, bah une écharpe, très bien.* ("A gift idea? I don't know, a scarf? Does she wear scarves? Great, a scarf it is then, very good.")

Michelin-Starred Restaurants

When it comes to food, Parisians are no experts. Most did not grow up with a mother cooking epic food. Parisian mothers usually have no time, interest, or money to invest in glorious cookery. Most Parisians grew up with what, from a French perspective, would be fair to call mediocre food on their plate.

The appetite for good food usually comes later in the Parisian's life. When the Parisian starts being able to afford eating out or traveling to *la province.* At that point only does he start exploring real cuisine, be it generous or refined.

Most active Parisians eat out regularly. But very few meals in a lifetime make it to the pantheon of memories. Very few meals leave an impression that never vanishes. Michelin-starred restaurants belong to that category. They offer grandiose moments, unforgettable ones.

Parisians like the idea of *artisans.* Given that, in the Parisian mind, a good artisan needs to be either broke or at the top of his profession. Artisans who make a reasonable living bother Parisians, who then think the artisans make too much money. Being broke shows passion and a form of charming inadequacy to the modern world that the Parisian is truly fond of. Being recognized by all shows that the summits of a craft have been reached. That is a pleasant thought: the Parisian could use a glimpse of that. Though Parisian chefs are usually looked down upon, Michelin-starred chefs are revered. To justify the sudden upgrade, the Parisian will usually drop the A-bomb. *Oui mais attention, pour moi, les grands chefs sont des artistes.* It is best at this stage not to start questioning the Parisian about how he considers other artists and the amount of money they are making.

Michelin-starred experiences are rare. They are the beacons of moments to remember. A Michelin-starred meal comes with a whole set of mental constructions, made up of food mythology, chef legend, and social glorification. It is about building up. Most Parisians will therefore always feel a form of discomfort in these restaurants. Thinking that it is too much, that they don't really belong there—in the heart of the legend. Treating a Parisian with a very nice meal is a tricky decision, as most will be unable to truly enjoy perfection of the service, beauty of the room, grace of the food, and enchantment of the wine—simply because *c'est trop.* Traces of a Catholic culture spark in the most unsuspected environments.

At the end of the meal, Parisians feel like they passed a test. They are relieved. They, too, somehow enjoyed themselves. Having been to a Michelin-starred restaurant once before propels the Parisian to a world of increased self-confidence. He, too, can now look forward to reading the new classification every year.

If at some point during the meal, the chef came out to salute the clients, the Parisian will use that second of interaction to his advantage for the rest of his life. He will refer to the chef as a good old friend in every conversation about gastronomy. Thus gaining much social precedence over his fellow Parisians. Which, all things considered, sheds a new light on the value of that meal.

USEFUL TIP: Should you want to sound like a pro, use the word *macarons* instead of *étoiles* ("stars"). Also, if you're on a tight budget, go for lunch (and reserve in advance).

SOUND LIKE A PARISIAN: *La Tour d'Argent, eh bah dis donc. . . . Quoique, il paraît qu'ils ont perdu une étoile. Oh tu me raconteras. . . .* ("La Tour d'Argent, well, look at you. . . . Though I heard they lost a star. You'll let me know how it was. . . .")

La Bretagne

Some places don't want to give themselves away. Their beauty lies in a cocoon, protected against the aggressions of the many. Some places remain shy despite their splendor. More aware of their flaws than of their qualities. Some places impose greatness in sobriety, they play silent symphonies. Some places shape people more so than people could ever shape them.

La Bretagne (also known as Brittany) is all this.

This region is a root, a flower, and a horizon. It is a castle and a breeze. It is the gray and the humble, the blue and the silent, the green and the painful. It inhabits its people. Its wind thickens the soul; its rain pervades hopes.

Easiness does not belong in Bretagne. Everything there comes at a price. Liking Bretagne is not about enjoying its beauty but about cherishing that price. This region of infinite humility can distinguish minds and souls as much as it can shatter them. Bretagne lovers are people of persistence. They are loyal to its defects to sometimes be privileged enough to enjoy its treasures. The immediateness of its rain fades away before the promise of its sun.

Parisians all fall for the superior beauty of the place. They all, too, fall for the idea of them loving Bretagne. Loving that gray and that rain, loving the cold and the unfriendly, loving the brutality of a character defined day after day by the unstoppable winds. Not all Parisians can take Bretagne. Unchained sunshines and insolent blues are reachable enough. They are easy enough. It takes a form of impermeability to the modern world to prefer the grays of Bretagne over them. Only poets can come back to Bretagne regularly, only they can cope with its superb attitude.

Most Parisians are deeply certain they love Bretagne. Yet very few go there repeatedly: *Attends, je bosse comme un dingue, je veux pas retrouver à passer un weekend sous la pluie, ah non, no way.* Rain it seems drenches even the most poetic of souls.

The gray skies of Bretagne let us contemplate that, observing this end of a land, one might also catch sight of the end of a world.

USEFUL TIP: The coastline of Bretagne is regularly breathtaking. Explore.

SOUND LIKE A PARISIAN: *Ah non, la Bretagne c'est magnifique, j'aime trop. Par contre les Bretons, qu'est-ce qu'ils picolent!* ("Oh no, Brittany is magnificent. I really love it. But the locals drink so much!")

Friendly Old People

Parisians have a bad image of old people. Most Parisians consider them useless, slow, and vaguely senile. Modern individualism and urban life have untied the link that once existed in families between generations, so it will come as no surprise that not caring enough for your own elderly makes it difficult to cope with the others. For most Parisians, the ancestral wisdom guarded by older folks is no longer worth listening to. The world has changed too much, they think.

Interestingly enough, while older folks are very keen to testify how much the world has changed, they seem to ignore that their own country has gone through a dramatic makeover during the past forty years. All the values, principles, and beliefs that made France a world power for a few centuries have been purely and simply flushed. Over honor, Parisians now prefer respect; over patriotism, antiracism; over Christianity, atheism; over work, creation; over dignity, self-fulfillment. . . . In that context, advice from the elderly certainly fails to resonate. Outdated.

The modern French society of respect has awkwardly banned politeness from the cardinal values that make up the decent man. In the fascinating early twenty-first century French social microclimate, respect seems to do well without politeness. In Paris, friendliness and joie de vivre are concepts that exist exclusively in the mind of candid tourists and some old people.

Friendly Parisians are to be found in two sociological groups: people working in the food business and old people. Since professionals can always be suspected of being friendly in order to attract more business, pure disinterested friendliness is only found in interactions with some older people.

Parisians like these moments. They like to see a joyful older person. They find that *super.* They love to have a little banter with a friendly old person at the *boulangerie* or *chez le fromager.* This reassures them and puts joy in their heart. Parisians have found the explanation for the friendliness of these elderly folks: they have more time, they don't have to work and therefore have it easy. The Parisian, on the other hand, has things to do, and therefore no time or energy to be friendly or polite.

It makes sense.

Friendly old people are also usually well put together. Parisians find them *trop mignon.* The elegance and lightheartedness they like to display is enough to touch the younger Parisian but certainly not to inspire him.

What good could they teach young Parisians anyway?

USEFUL TIP: Old French people love being smiled at.

SOUND LIKE A PARISIAN: *Y avait une p'tite vieille à la boulangerie, toute gentille, qui m'a dit que j'avais un joli sourire. Tu me dis pas toi, hein, que j'ai un joli sourire?!* ("There was this old woman in the bakery, very sweet: she told me I had a beautiful smile. You never tell me I have a beautiful smile!")

La Fleur de Sel

When it comes to salting food, salt is good enough for most people, but Parisians can't help thinking there has to be something better. Thankfully, there is: the Rolls-Royce of salt, *la fleur de sel.*

The single most highly prized salt on earth, gently raked by hand, in a gesture inherited from time, to capture only the finest flakes floating on the surface of the marshes.

A real Parisian is to own three types of salt: *du gros sel, du sel,* and *de la fleur de sel.* Gradation of refinement. *Le gros sel* will do wonders to saltwater, *le sel* will salt ingredients. *La fleur de sel,* however, will vastly exceed its salting atributes. It will crown a recipe, a presentation, and a social status. The fact that it is a much better quality salt, softer on the palate, visually satisfying, and mildly crunchy is secondary.

Buying *fleur de sel* is making a statement. You are a gourmet and spending much more for quality is something you are willing to do (even more so as—conveniently enough—we're just talking salt). *Fleur de sel* is one of these things the Parisian is happy to buy and display yet rarely use. One of these delicacies he feels he should save for a more precious occasion, or for a more precisely executed dish.

Among all the *fleurs de sel* available, the Parisian will surely opt for *la fleur de sel de Guérande.* In a conversation about salt in Paris, the name *Guérande* will be dropped after usually less than ten seconds. No matter how common the reference is, the Parisian will still think of himself as an insider for bringing it up.

La fleur de sel is an unusual flower. As with all flowers, it takes water and sunshine to bring it to life. But while most flowers satisfy the nose and the heart, *la fleur de sel* takes care of the palate and the mind. If most people wish for a bit more salt in their lives, it is fair to say that Parisians often hope for more *fleur de sel.* As if a bit more of the simple were to bring a bit of simple to the more.

USEFUL TIP: Reserve *la fleur de sel* for the final touch on your cooking.

SOUND LIKE A PARISIAN: *Hop, un peu de fleur de sel . . . et voilà! C'est beau non?* ("Hop, a bit of *fleur de sel* . . . there you go! Pretty, don't you think?")

La Place des Vosges

Paris is a city of axes and perspectives. Its most glorious avenues, monuments, parks, and boulevards do not happen to be there by chance. This organization has been designed and orchestrated century after century by men with an idea of *grandeur.*

While the Parisian likes the tortuous and winding streets, he also likes to navigate reassured through his city, sensing the layers of accumulated greatness. Paris is a delightful city for it seems to know the human soul. It knows its need for beauty and its need for greatness. It knows its need for space and its need for intricacies. It knows its need for perspectives and that for projections. In Paris, the grown-up soul feels at home.

Parisians take credit for this unique greatness. All the arrogance the city chooses never to display, the Parisian has long internalized. Spoiled little children, certain that their parents' talents and accomplishments were passed on to their genes. Precedence of their soul.

Some places manage to combine greatness and modesty. In these places, one can hear stentorian whispers. Architectural perfection fades under the perfect suns of the human soul deciphered. La Place des Vosges is such. Obscenely square and fully self-centered yet surprisingly convivial and truly welcoming. The formal harmony of the place does not oppress the

visitor. *Au contraire.* It frees him. No matter how busy, Parisian, or preoccupied one may be, walking into la Place des Vosges, he becomes a visitor: he gets caught in the local pace, captured in the microclimate. This square turns people into *promeneurs.* Entering this square, they leave dirty Bastille and self-important Marais behind. They access a new reality, enriched with an ambition that those gifted with sight would not dare to question.

There is a form of immodesty in posing as less than one is. La Place des Vosges, however, asserts its modesty by imposing its greatness. The park at the center of the place follows the same pattern. It does not mean to enchant or to soothe. Consequently, it does. This square is fully congruent. And Parisians feel that. They like to loll around under the archways. Looking at the art. Resting on a bench. Observing life pass by in this odd carrousel.

Feeling little for a moment.

USEFUL TIP: If you like squares, check out nearby Place du Marché Sainte Catherine. Quiet different but charming.

SOUND LIKE A PARISIAN: *J'crois que sa famille a un appart' sur la Place des Vosges. . . . Non non, beaucoup d'argent. Beaucoup, beaucoup d'argent.* ("I believe that her family has an apartment on la Place des Vosges. . . . No, lots of money. Lots and lots of money.")

Not Talking About Their Money

Legend has it that the French are not comfortable talking about money.

Wrong.

They are not comfortable talking about their money. Their money is no one's business but their own. Oddly enough, that rule does not seem to apply to others: Parisians quite enjoy talking about other people's money. While they do enjoy the usual *miserabiliste* bit on how poor some people are, Parisians are keen to move on rapidly to a crunchier conversation: that of how absurdly rich some people are. Parisians are fascinated with wealthy people. They revere them as much as they hate them. Once dissipated, the smokes of scorn unveil admiration (the reverse is equally true).

On top of the scandalously rich pyramid are two types of people: *les banquiers* and *les footballeurs.* There is little doubt that these men steal their money. Over the past few years, the acceptance level has grown for sports players' earnings, but has dropped for bankers' earnings. Parisians are somewhat more tolerant with entrepreneurs who struck it rich, but they, too, should behave and keep a low profile. After all, the Parisian can always pull the exploitation card.

Parisians love to talk about scandalously wealthy people, as they very well know that they never will be. It is easier to despise what is fully foreign. Left-wing Parisians abide by Notorious BIG's words: "Mo' money, mo' problems." The more lucid ones know the French business context and taxmen too well to even start considering enjoying significant amounts of money one day. Ultimately, only one type of Parisian finds himself comfortable talking about money: the Parisian who lives overseas. Not all Parisians living overseas become comfortable talking about money. Those who do usually don't come back.

Parents and spouses are the only ones able to rejoice about someone's dramatic increase in revenue. No Parisian will ever wish wealth or financial success to another being. Not because he might suspect that wealth is not necessarily the path to happiness, but simply because the Parisian would like for no one's revenues to exceed his too significantly. That is his policy.

While Anglo magazines thrive on ranking companies based on various criteria, French ones rank indiviuals' based on their wealth. The special *"Classement des Français les plus riches"* attracts enough readers to be on the cover of most mainstream magazines at least once a year. It is important for Parisians to stay on top of such crucial information. Knowing who has not abided by his policy.

When it comes to the money they earn, Parisians have a rule: it is not enough. Mostly because it is less than their boss's (right-wing Parisian) and less than what the company's profit would allow (left-wing Parisian).

Talking about money in Paris is considered rude. Money in Paris is a vulgar thing. Spending it to make life easier is acceptable. Spending it to make it too distinctly enjoyable is not. Spending your life struggling with it is acceptable. Spending your life not struggling with it is not. In Paris, discretion and decency should preside over any decision or conversation involving money. Anyone enjoying the money he earned will immediately be called a *nouveau riche.* Until the Parisian gets to benefit from it, at which point the person will be deemed as *hyper généreux.*

Though kings and queens were beheaded an odd two hundred years ago, courtesans still prosper in Paris. With discretion and decency of course.

USEFUL TIP: Keeping a Parisian friend implies skipping most money-related subjects, except for those about insufficient revenues.

SOUND LIKE A PARISIAN: *C'est le fils je crois qui a fait fortune. Dans la constrction, ou la restauration, aux Etats-Unis je crois. Enfin, bref, le type est plein aux as et il s'est acheté une baraque incroyable dans le Lubéron. Enfin, tu vois le genre, quoi. . . .* ("I believe it's the son who struck it rich. In construction, or in the restaurant business, maybe. Well, he was in America. Anyway, they guy is super loaded and he bought himself a stunning house in the Lubéron. I mean, you get the drift. . . .")

Sunglasses

The sun rarely shines in Paris. But when it does, the Parisian intends to enjoy life. After all the gray he's gone through, he feels entitled to a vacation. On a generously sunny day, he will thus unilaterally decide to leave work early and he will wear sunglasses.

A few years ago, sunglasses were considered out of place in Paris. People wearing them were mocked and pointed at. Ridiculous show-offs. A form of nobility existed then in facing the sun, remaining strong, eyes half closed, enduring its attacks.

Things have changed. In Paris, the sun is now to be embraced. Not confronted, but instead dated. Sunglasses are a Parisian's most precious asset in his ephemeral flings with the sun. With them on, the Parisian can fully enjoy. Enjoyment in Paris is no longer about dignified confrontation, but about enjoyment.

The choice of his pair of sunglasses is a very difficult decision to make for the Parisian. *Fashion? Pas trop fashion? Marron? Noir? Ecailles, pas écailles? Trop rondes? Pas assez rondes?* Modern dilemmas are breathtaking. The Parisian wearing sunglasses is unable to buy a non-branded pair. Walking the streets of Paris with a pair with no logo on it would be straight-up shameful. Sunglasses should help increase a Parisian's comfort, not diminish it. Most Parisians cannot afford Christian Dior couture. So Christian Dior glasses will do: *un petit luxe* . . . The satisfaction about today's consumption of luxury brands is no longer about being able to afford them or differentiate yourself with them—just the opposite. It's about pretending and blending in. After all, the Parisian may indeed be more blinded than he thinks.

What matters in the end about the Parisians' sunglasses is the size of the logo. The more discreet the logo, the more elegant the sunglasses will be deemed. The more flashy, the more *nouveau riche* or *beauf*. Each brand comes with its own mythology and associated social values. Depending on the social class and personal history of each Parisian, such mythologies and associated values will vary. Making the sunglasses scene an eminently controversial one in Paris.

USEFUL TIP: Save your money.

SOUND LIKE A PARISIAN: *Le mec tu vois, chemises blanche, cheveux en arrière, Ray-Bans . . . la totale quoi!* ("That guy was like white shirt, hair pulled back, Ray-Bans . . . the total package!")

Saying *Trop*

Trop in French is "too much."

Previous generations used the word to indicate things that were in excess; excess was usually bad: *il est trop gros, il en fait trop, il parle trop, c'est trop chaud . . . Trop* was beyond reason or beyond acceptable limits. It was by no means an enviable adverb.

The past few years have brought about a tremendous shift in the way the word was used in Paris. The younger generation has taken it over and injected a new meaning and mystique to it. That generation of moderation, deprived of character, indulging with no joy in opulence turned *trop* into a laudatory term.

Trop became a marker of enthusiasm. In an ocean of unexcitement, language became their ultimate buoy. Young Parisians started using *trop* to express favorable impressions: *c'est trop bien, il est trop beau, elle a trop la classe. Très, super*, and *hyper* were no longer enough. Cool was to be found in self-proclaimed excess. Needless to say that excess—the judge of it being young Parisians, hence most likely a being with little joviality or ability to ever explore it—in that case has nothing to do with the object of the *trop*.

While *trop* switched from meaning "too much" to meaning "very much," its use grew more positive. *Je suis trop content*;

MAIRIE DE PARIS
10523

oh, ça me fait trop envie . . . Paris started flourishing with *trops*. The phrase *il est trop* became a must for funny people or cute children. Parisians using *trop* in such a way try to look more enthusiastic about what they witness than they truly are. They try to come across as flabbergasted by things they usually can't really get excited about. *Trop* is trying to be polite and cool at the same time. It's about not seeming as depressed as you are.

This slow-motion shift of the definition of excess comforted Parisians in the idea that their reputation for being not fun was a myth. When everything in one's life is *trop*, moderation becomes a necessity. Little by little, concealing dullness turned into justifying moderation and therefore—at the end of the day—fostering more dullness.

Older Parisians find themselves quite upset when they hear *trop* used in that way. Feeling a form of disconnection with the youth. It is hard to blame them. A youth that forgets to have fun is difficult to relate to.

USEFUL TIP: As a foreigner, it's probably best not to go down this road.

SOUND LIKE A PARISIAN: *Non, c'était trop bien. Musique de ouf: trop de la balle!* ("No, it was very good. Great music: it was the bomb.")

English Humor

Seen from Paris, England does not seem like a very likable country. Parisians like to recite the long list of afflictions the old nemesis seems to have: bad weather, alcoholism, ugliness, revolting food, hooliganism. . . . There seems to be no redemption.

However, there is one aspect of English culture that Parisians look up to. Oddly enough, it is not a phenomenon but instead an actual fringe of English society: upper-class English people.

Parisians thrive on the mythology of the *vieux lord anglais* and its escort of enchanting adverbs and manners. This mythology feeds a tiny but indisputable inferiority complex rooted in the prestigious mystique of England's academic institutions. It is clear to all Parisians that England shapes its elite better than France does. The legend of Eton, Cambridge, and Oxford is undoubtedly more vibrant in Paris than it could ever be in the UK.

Parisians all wish they could have English humor. They revere the inherent distinction, discreet wisdom, and smiley distance that come in the English humor package; add the English true *gourmandise* in the choice of the words and you'll find the Parisian irremediably charmed. In good English company, the world seems to be freed from triviality.

Though Parisians proclaim as often as they can their indefectible love for English humor, most cannot deal too well with absurdity. As much as reality can be disturbing, Parisians have a hard time resolving themselves to let go of it for a second. This relationship to reality explains that characters like Benny Hill or Mr. Bean do not gather unanimous support in Paris.

On the topic of English humor, Parisians rarely refrain from using the adjective *pince-sans-rire.* They are somehow jealous of that trait of English culture that allows its people to be intelligent and fun at the same time. They wished they, too, could juggle with humor and wit and be socially rewarded for it.

But it is too late. Paris has drenched the spark in most eyes. Humor is a mental exercise the city does not foster. Thus reinforcing Parisians in their vision that the bridge between them and upper-class English simply cannot be bridged. This vaguely depressing and resignated thought satisfies the Parisian.

So much for wanting to be humorous.

USEFUL TIP: To make Parisian friends, don't bother trying to adopt French humor (French what?). English is the way to go.

SOUND LIKE A PARISIAN: *Oh, Hugh Grant j'adore! Le côté très british, élégant, très fin, pince-sans-rire: excellent!* ("Oh, I love Hugh Grant! The whole elegant British type, very intelligent, tongue-in-cheek: excellent!")

Barcelona

Barcelona is the coolest city in the world. This Parisian truth is not negotiable.

Over the past decade, Barcelona has become a prime destination for a weekend break for most Parisians. Parisians like what the rest of Europeans do, starting with the fun atmosphere and the great weather. Parisians enjoy Barcelona all the more so as Paris and Barcelona share many characteristics. They are the business capitals of their countries and boast global appeal and reputation.

But because Barcelona is in Spain, Parisians cannot resolve themselves to look up to it. They can certainly recognize its impressive accomplishments, fantastic energy, and apparent wealth. This knowledge that the city is populated by overachievers makes the Parisian feel very much at ease there. Many Parisians claim to love Barcelona's creative, hipster vibe and certainly do. But this energy can only thrive in a city that can afford coolness. Barcelona certainly can and Parisians love that about it.

Understanding the extraordinary reputation that Barcelona has in Paris takes grasping fully the superior bind that exists between Parisians and Barcelona. One, for the record, they are vastly oblivious to. Barcelona is the capital of Catalonia. Its population vastly looks down on the rest of the country that in return generously dislikes them. The city is probably the country's most appealing metropolis yet fails to charm other Spaniards, who see in it nothing but arrogance. Parisians can relate to that. They, too, feel like they are the fuel to the country's engine and would like some signs of appreciation from the little people that make up the rest of the population.

Parisians like people that can resist. As such, they appreciate Catalonia's fierce action in favor of their language, culture, and identity. They admire a group of people that can stand for what it believes in. A group of individuals that still believes in some things, even more so in concepts that in Paris are no longer in fashion, like cultural identity. Catalans are still holding strong to things Parisians have long given up on. In that they can look up to them; Parisians can relate to them.

When visiting Barcelona, most Parisians cannot help but think that they could see themselves living there. They will predominantly talk about the weather, the quality of life, and the energy. They will also mention the bars and the nightlife.

Clearly, the sun might be shining a bit too hard in Barcelona.

USEFUL TIP: Preferring any other Spanish city will make you seem old.

SOUND LIKE A PARISIAN: *Et dans quinze jours, on va à Barcelone pour le weekend: trop bien, j'ai trop hâte.* ("And in two weeks, we're off to Barcelona for the weekend: can't wait.")

Reasonably Boring Nightlife

When asked by tourists or foreigners to recommend a good place to go out at night, Parisians find themselves quite annoyed. Older folks will come up with a general-enough statement, fully certain that destinations like Champs-Elysées or Bastille have everything the fun-minded *noctambule* might hope for.

Younger Parisians whose experience of nightlife is more recent and more frequent know such answers are not really helpful. Should they name neighborhoods, they would probably opt for Saint-Germain or Oberkampf. Things get more complicated when asked to name cool bars or fun clubs. Most Parisians are vastly clueless about good places to go out at night in Paris.

This phenomenon has to do with the patterns of Parisian entertainment. Parisians like to meet up with friends. They do so at house parties, dinner parties, or dinners out. In the summertime, they are also prone to do picnics and *apéros.* Except for house parties, food is—if not the central element—at least the main excuse and environment for Parisian fun. A good evening is one with good friends, and food.

Though the trend is on the way up, drinking for the sake of it is not a central element of French culture.

A nice meal is one that takes the time to drag on. It finishes in a state and at a time that can easily excuse tiresome. At that point, transitioning from a Parisian restaurant to a club vibe or a bar is certainly not the natural thing to do.

Another explanation for the difficulties most Parisian have in naming good places to go is the fact that such places are scarce. The festive ways of la Belle Epoque, the liberated excesses of *la génération '68* are long gone. While the practice explained above has always existed, Parisians were once more jolly. Most Parisians these days do not feel like partying, many cannot afford it, and the result is—in comparison to what may exist in other international capitals—a reasonably boring nightlife.

For Parisians, naming a good place for a fun night out is all the more difficult as it requires going out. Most young Parisians are in relationships, so the appeal of going out vanishes vastly as going out becomes a threat more than an opportunity. When they do go out, Parisians have a secret rule to stick to their friends. Groups arrive constituted and leave similarly constituted. After a few nights out in Paris, most outsiders start complaining about the difficulties of mixing and mingling with Parisians, even in bars and clubs.

Arrogant little things . . . thinking that Parisians could have any interest or find any pleasure in interacting with them. . . .

USEFUL TIP: Fancy clubs in Paris are difficult to get into: wait until at least midnight, be dressed up, avoid coming in large groups, and make sure you have at least one girl for every guy in your party.

SOUND LIKE A PARISIAN: *Oulah, et ils veulent danser?! Pff . . . j'sais pas moi. Marie, t'as une idée? Pour aller danser? Hein, nan, hein, j'sais pas . . . Saint-Germain c'est sympa, non?* ("Oh boy, and they want to dance?! Pff . . . I know I don't. Marie, do you know where to go dancing? I don't know . . . Saint-Germain is OK, right?")

Testosterone-Deprived Males

There are three types of males in Paris: the gay-looking homosexuals, the gay-looking heterosexuals, and men over fifty.

It is not easy being over fifty in Paris. Most men over fifty happen not to look gay, which screams that they are obviously one generation behind. They have no choice but to accept that situation for it is difficult to start looking gay after a few decades of looking straight.

Parisian males under fifty do not have such problems. They can happily look gay and have no one cast suspect that they are on the wrong side of the age hill. In Paris, gay men find themselves looking or acting gay and it is only fair. What is more surprising to the visitor is that the same pattern applies to the nongay Parisian male—who also finds himself looking and acting gay in most situations of life.

The first rule of a good Parisian male body is puniness. This objective is reached thanks to years of not exercising and not playing any sports at a competitive level. Add years of not drinking or eating in excess and the puniness grail can be reached.

To cover their glorious bodies, Parisian males opt for clothes that rank somewhere between neutral and gay-looking. The beauty of a neutral piece of clothing on a puny body is that it immediately becomes gay-looking. It is crucial to realize that, whether they choose to wear neutral or gay-looking clothes, heterosexual Parisian males do not have the intention to look gay. They look *bien, normal.*

Acting gay follows a similar pattern. While some homosexual males act gay for understandable reasons, visitors might be astonished at how gay heterosexual Parisian males usually act. Acting gay is to some extent a recent French habit, inherited from three decades of institutionalization of a cotton-candied, pacified vision of the world and of humans as a species. But once again, Parisians take this to the next level: when most French males outside Paris act gay on certain topics only, Parisians choose to go all the way. The concept of being "a real man" is vastly looked down upon for displaying far too obviously characteristics that relate to a lack of intelligence and refinement: concepts like strength, masculinity, physical power, and strong opinions or values are therefore very preoccupying in Paris. They are viewed as an open door to brutality.

At this point, one may feel compassion for the Parisian woman. Well, one should save his compassion for gay Parisian men. Gay Parisian men are probably the only people in Paris longing to see more testosterone around them. They should be the subjects of one's compassion. Parisian men are happy to think of themselves as beyond activities and behaviors that attest of a form of masculinity. As far as they're concerned, Parisian women do not necessarily know any better. If their boyfriend looks gay, it is primarily because *c'est un mec hyper sympa, très fin, vraiment intelligent.* Parisian woman have grown so wise that they have overcome their natural inclinations. Masculine is coarse and rough. End of the story. The idea that a male human could be masculine as well as being a refined person is not one *la Parisienne* is ready to embrace.

Indeed, examples of such phenomena in Paris are rare enough to assume that the rule of Paris is probably the rule of nature.

USEFUL TIP: Do not be fooled: looking and acting gay does not equal being gay.

SOUND LIKE A PARISIAN: *J'suis allé faire un peu de shopping: un p'tit t-shirt col V, des p'tites lunettes Kenzo et des espadrilles. Tranquille, quoi, pour l'été* . . . ("I went shopping: a little T-shirt with a V-neck, Kenzo sunglasses, and espadrilles . . . Sweet, just summer gear . . .")

Le Dalaï-Lama

The modern world deprives its people of real heroes. The entertainment, sports, and media industries do their very best to provide idols for the people they occupy. But these frequently lack the spiritual dimension that makes the real hero. A real hero has to be both spiritual and political. He resists the established powers and fights for his ideas.

Le Dalaï-Lama is one of the world's only heroes. No Parisian would ever contest this fact. All Parisians are very much fond of him. His chubby face and benevolent smile make for a reassuring persona: the charming resistance against the tyranny of a faceless oppressor. His cause is the most just of all and the Parisian is a just person. He is always very prone to sign petitions against tyranny. Especially Chinese tyranny, which he doesn't care for too much. He has the courage to tell his friends in France how appalling he finds the attitude of the Chinese government. He sometimes pushes courage as far as to threaten to boycott Chinese products. He rarely follows suit, though, because "it's not what it's about." But such threats are very, very scary.

Interestingly enough, the Parisian, no matter how much he is into freedom of mind and against propaganda, rarely bothers to double-check his facts. He remains vastly foreign to elements that might otherwise feed and qualify his reflection.

Knowing, for instance—among other elements that can easily be looked up—that Tibetan Buddhism is the latest of all forms of Buddhism, that as such le Dalaï-Lama is the pope only to an odd 1 percent of the world's Buddhists, that a country ruled by monks has rarely freed him from religious obscurantism, that most Buddhists live in China where they are by no means persecuted . . . is not on the Parisian's agenda.

Le Dalaï-Lama is good. China is bad. Amen.

On the topic of le Dalaï-Lama, as with most of those having to do with politics, disagreeing with the Parisian's views is a dangerous thing to do. That will classify you—not as subversive—but instead as right wing. If your opinion is susceptible to reach a significant number of people through a given media, Parisians will start a petition against you.

It is best to behave really. . . .

USEFUL TIP: Having an interest in Buddhism will impress most Parisians.

SOUND LIKE A PARISIAN: *Attends, mais quand tu vois ce que font les Chinois au Tibet, moi ça me révolte, j'veux dire. . . . D'ailleurs y a un concert de soutien organisé en juin. Ca te branche?* ("Wait, but when you see what the Chinese do in Tibet, I'm revolted, I have to say. . . . Oh, by the way, there's a big concert in June to support the Tibetan cause. Are you interested?")

Interns

Forget about money, nice suits, and company cars. The real treasure of a Parisian professional life is interns.

Stagiaires, as they're known in French, have become the cornerstone of business life in Paris. Interns fulfill two main functions in a Parisian office: they take care of the office's dullest or most painstaking tasks and they bring sexual tension to the workplace.

Le stagiaire is always *motivé,* as (s)he likes to repeat in interviews. He works hard *pour faire ses preuves.* For his dedication and hard work, the intern is compensated generously with a hefty monthly check (usually around 400 euros [U.S.$500] per month for a full-time internship) and the right to add the name of the company to his résumé. For companies, interns are a glorious invention combining ridiculous pay and unrivaled obedience. Hard to beat.

All the more so as his position is filled by a new person every three to six months, since interns are rarely hired at the end of the internship. This keeps the workplace exciting for the unhappily married or sexually frustrated ones. *T'as vu la nouvelle stagiaire?* is a question that does not necessarily refer to the competence of the new intern.

Most French students will do at least three internships before graduating. *Le stage* has become a new French institution and *le stagiaire* the key to France's remarkable productivity. The French job market is so highly dysfunctional it is almost charming to witness it from overseas. "Oh, the French . . ." Take the prohibitive cost of labor, spice it up with a vague impossibility to fire an employee, and sprinkle it with the culture of conflict and defiance employees have toward employers . . . let that macerate for a few years and you'll reach a country with a steady (read minimal) 10 percent unemployment rate. The solutions to the problems are quite obvious and well known but would require a form of political courage. It is therefore best not to count on it.

The unemployment rate among French kids under twenty-five years old is above 25 percent. The oh-so-brave French politicians claim they want to tackle this problem. They probably will. It doesn't take too much imagination to know that their idea will be to increase the cost of hiring interns and to make it impossible to fire bad interns.

As with most things in Paris, there exists a hierarchy in the quality of the intern. Extremely good-looking interns score high points, along with graduates of a French *grande école*. Ultimate victory will go to having as an intern a graduate from Oxford, Cambridge, or an American Ivy League. The most precise indicator of professional success in Paris is quite simple: really successful professionals do not have interns. They have *une assistante*.

Their *assistante*, of course, has an intern.

USEFUL TIP: All French companies hire interns: all you need is a student visa. Speaking French is, of course, preferable.

SOUND LIKE A PARISIAN: *J'ai un nouveau stagiaire qui arrive en mai; J'ai hâte là parce celui qu'on se traîne depuis janvier est une chèvre. Je suis complètement sous l'eau en ce moment.* ("I'll have a new intern starting in May. Can't wait as the one we currently have is a complete catastrophe. I'm swamped with work right now.")

Expats

When it comes to professional life, Parisians find themselves in a catch-22. They want the seriousness that makes a real job. And the sense of adventure that makes a real life.

Needless to say, such positions are hard to obtain.

"Real job" for Parisians implies either a corporate job or working for a prestigious institution. All other jobs are not serious. "Real life" implies the possibility of sailing a boat on the weekend and exposure to other cultures, while of course enjoying an eminently comfortable lifestyle.

Given these parameters, it will come as no surprise that Parisians love expats. Being an expat brings the best of both worlds: a good, well-paid position in a foreign yet cozy environment. Bingo!

Parisians would all like at some point in their career to be sent overseas on an expat contract. Since these days—as Parisians like to complain—*ils ne font plus de contrats d'expat,* many Parisians are given opportunities overseas on a *contrat local.* This option is acceptable for Parisians under thirty-five and for destinations where salaries are significant. If these two conditions are not met, chances are the Parisian is more into real life than real job. Expat contracts having become scarce, and those who obtain them tend to be on the efficient side and are therefore probably more into real jobs.

While Parisians look up to their fellow Parisians who go exploring on a mission, they do enjoy the possibility to socialize with foreign expats. Having an expat friend displays fantastic *ouverture internationale* and implies that the Parisian is both a gracious host and possibly a polyglot. Talking about his expat friend, the Parisian will always mention his nationality: *"Tu sais, Mark, mon copain expat canadien."* He will also make mention of the quality of his position: *"Il a un très gros poste chez Microsoft . . . un type assez brillant vraiment."* The Parisian will always compliment his expat friend publicly on his French: *"Non, vraiment, il parle très bien. Non, c'est vrai Mark, tu as fait de gros progrès."* The Parisian doesn't think Mark's French is any good but he likes to come across as the benevolent paternalist mentor.

Having an expat friend is about adding glow to the Parisian's life. Not all countries come with the same glamorous touch. Having an American expat friend is the ultimate luxury, then comes South American, then other Anglo countries, then Italy. Having expat friends from any other country will only be acceptable in left-wing circles for whom the betrayal of having friends in the corporate world (losers) will be compensated by the unlikeliness of their country of origin.

Expats arriving in Paris are usually very keen to make Parisian friends and to work on their French. Soon enough, they give up on French and, not long after, on Parisians. Those who love the city enough end up re-creating a Parisian life with compatriots, other international folks, and Parisians who have lived abroad long enough. Those who don't just leave—disenchanted.

For Parisians with social ambitions, the proportion of expats and foreigners at the events they organize is the safest way not only to attract Parisians of quality but also to place themselves on a nice international pedestal—with both their expat and Parisian friends.

Interestingly enough, in Paris, the quality of a social circle will be judged predominantly on the proportion of its internationals. The higher the proportion, the more desirable the circle.

Having many international friends helps Parisians overcome their catch-22. They keep their serious job, while getting a taste of adventure through their international friends. Between real job and real life, Parisians choose not to choose: they opt for real Parisian life.

USEFUL TIP: Expats should not be shy about talking to Parisians. They will usually be very much welcome.

SOUND LIKE A PARISIAN: *Je peux venir avec mon copain expat? Tu sais, l'Américain, de Boston . . . tu vas voir, il est très sympa.* ("May I come with my expat friend? You know, the American from Boston . . . you'll see, he's great.")

100%
PARISIEN
APPROUVÉ

Les Droits de l'Homme

Parisians can tolerate many things. But there is one thing they are not ready to mess with. One thing that if you touch, you will get in big Parisian trouble. One holy thing, superior to all others: *les droits de l'homme* ("human rights").

Parisians are insanely into human rights. It is their alpha and their omega. The square to their circle. The divinity they all worship. Unfortunately, Parisians have grown to believe that France was *le pays des droits de l'homme.* This modest belief, probably rooted in the French revolution's Déclaration des Droits de l'Homme et du Citoyen in 1789 makes France morally responsible for any attempt against human rights on the planet. The French have to intervene, thus annoying most other countries who view as arrogance what the French view as generosity. That Plato, Marcus Aurelius, the Old Testament, Saint Paul, the Habeas Corpus, the Bill of Rights, Bartolomé de la Casas, or George Mason were all anterior to the French Revolution does not seem to bother Parisians. That the United Nations adopted la Déclaration Universelle des Droits de l'Homme in 1945 doesn't either. Human rights is a French concept and France should in that matter be the lawyer, the judge, and the sheriff.

Parisians in their utter courage are always prone to *dénoncer toute atteinte aux droits de l'homme.* They will protest by signing petitions, attending free concerts, wearing provocative T-shirts, and even, sometimes, joining *des manifestations de soutien* ("support protests"—a very French concept). All these are extremely helpful. Because it is extremely left wing, the French media thrives on the concept of *droits de l'homme.* In the sneakiest of ways, they present most things they disagree with as *une atteinte aux droits de l'homme.* Beautifully enough, according to the French media, France is probably the country in the world where attacks against human rights are the most shocking. Examples are countless and all generously criticized in the media: French prisons are dirty and overcrowded (*atteinte aux droits de l'homme*), illegal aliens are being sent back to their countries (*atteinte aux droits de l'homme*), some people are poor (*atteinte aux droits de l'homme*). . . .

The few Parisians left that sense in this disastrous *droits de l'hommisme* a form of vaguely pleasing option for the weak minds will be considered right wing and usually banned socially. *Le droit de l'hommisme* satisfies those deprived of realism, culture, and courage: it does wonders in Paris. In their utter knowledge of foreign cultures, Parisians feel like bragging overseas that their impotent flag has any impact on the policy of the Chinese, Russians, or Arabs. It is true that these people are probably quite annoyed with those free concerts. Instead of trying to reverse the trend of their dying influence and power, Parisians are happy to merely protest. Unfortunately, their ignorant and childish attitude is loud enough to resonate in a way that French politicians feel like they need to act on. Thus making France happily fall in the *droits de l'homme* well.

Interestingly enough, the same Parisians that protest against the unbearable attacks against human rights worldwide have no problem vacationing in Cuba or Myanmar. They are certainly bothered by the fact that some of the things they buy might be made by underpaid children in China or India but not to the point to rank that as *une atteinte aux droits de l'homme.* And it's only fair. For when you think about it, protesting against yourself might very well be *une atteinte aux droits de l'homme.*

USEFUL TIP: Not a tip, just a prayer for you Anglos out there. Please don't let this mentality take over all the West. Please. Also, read *The Camp of the Saints* by Jean Raspail. Great book.

SOUND LIKE A PARISIAN: *Attends, mais on est quand meme en France, c'est scandaleux. . . . On est quand meme le pays des droits de l'homme.* ("Wait, I mean we're in France. It's scandalous. . . . This is the human rights country, this can't be happening.")

Le Métro

Parisians and their metro are an old couple. After years of frequenting each other daily, they know each other inside and out. On a good day, they manage to realize how precious they are to one another. On a bad day, every little hitch will make the presence of the other unbearable.

The metro is not jealous: for most Parisians, the metro has been the moving theater of fleeting passions and poetic rifts. Every decent Parisian has fallen in love several times in the metro—complete strangers becoming in those enchanted tunnels the subjects of ephemeral infatuations. Those six-minute love stories—mute and delicious. For hopeless romantics, line 1 in the spring or summer is like a gift from heaven. Is it a fashion show? Nope, it's the metro. When it comes to people watching, Parisians know that cafés are overrated: the metro is the real deal. Geared up with a book or an iPod, the Parisian is ready to explore otherness with discretion.

The choice of entertainment accessory will help brush up the Parisian's metro profile. An iPod will make him appear like another sheep while a book will make him look smart. The choice of the book is crucial: mainstream books and current bestsellers are to be avoided—vulgar. Edginess is good but should not be pushed too far. The safest and most refined option is going with a classic. Playing the *décalé* card is also an option: cartoons for twelve-year-olds are always a big hit for the dandy. The killer trick, the ultimate book remaining is *Le Petit Prince*—the prettiest, single most elegant invitation to living a beautiful life. Pulling it out in the metro is like making a flower grow in a desert; it creates a moment.

At the end of the day, metro players are real romantics. The women that charm them rarely suspect how lovely they can make the journey, between Étoile and Rivoli.

Not all rides, though, constitute beautiful *parentheses enchantées* in a Parisian day. Some stimulate the Parisian's need to complain (unusually rightly so in that case): common topics usually have to do with odors, temperature, slowliness, punctuality, and the favorite of all: strikes. Parisians cannot stand metro strikes. On a strike day, they will systematically use the word *prise d'otages.* Line 14, which has the good taste of being fully automated, never goes on strike. It is as such many a Parisian's preferred line.

In all cases, the worst of all metro lines is still more enjoyable than the regional rail service. Those long trains are deeper, faster, and venture out to the suburbs. Exploring the depths of the region's public transportation system is a painful thought to most Parisians. They can handle heat, smells, and strikes, but really—not *banlieusards.*

Most of the time, the Paris metro happens to look like a world championship of depression on rails. *Provinciaux* love to pick on Parisians for that: *Oh, eh, vous faîtes tous la gueule, vous les Parisiens, dans le métro.* Fair enough. Two weeks after his arrival, it is good to know that a vast majority of *provinciaux* usually become serious contenders for a medal in this bucolic championship. When it comes to qualifying *le métro,* two adjectives have Parisians' preference: *pratique* and *rapide.*

Both apply quite well indeed. Though, to some Parisians, the balance of comfort outweights the *pratique et rapide* one. For them, two options remain: leaving Paris or buying a scooter.

Walking the streets of Paris and watching the countless scooters attests that no matter how much Parisians change, they are still more prone to take a new lover than to leave their old spouse.

USEFUL TIP: Get a credit card with a chip and ride a Vélib'.

SOUND LIKE A PARISIAN: *Tu prends la 4. Toc, trois stations et t'y es. Facile. Bon, on se voit ce soir. J'te fais la bise, je file, j'suis à la bourre . . .* ("You take the 4. Three stops and you're there. Easy. Good, I'll see you tonight. Have to run, I'm late . . .")

Le Chèvre Chaud

The most popular appetizer in Paris is *le chèvre chaud* ("warm goat cheese"). Several denominations may apply for it: *tartine de chèvre chaud, salade de chèvre chaud, croustillant de chèvre chaud* . . . but the concept is always the same: take fresh goat cheese, slice it thinly, place the slices on some bread, put it all in the oven for a little tanning session, and serve with green salad and vinaigrette.

The Parisians that are the most keen to order *chèvre chaud* are the ones *qui font attention*—understand, those who are concerned about their weight. For some very odd reason, most Parisians consider *chèvre chaud* to be very healthy. As if the presence of green salad, combined with the virginal whiteness of goat cheese and the grease-free contribution of the oven annihilated the fact that bread is still bread and cheese still cheese.

In terms of bread, two main options exist: the first one consists of putting one slice of cheese on each slice of bread. The bread in that case will be more of a crouton-style, usually from a baguette. The other option, which is also the most common, is a larger slice of bread, usually thinner, too. Drop the Poilâne name and it will seal the deal (Poilâne bread is one of the rare food products where gourmet Parisians accept to opt for name rather than taste).

Restaurateurs who have *grandes salades* on their menu will usually offer *une grande salade de chèvre chaud.* Still feminine as a salad should be, but substantial enough to a normal person (read not a *Parisienne*). The contrast of temperature reinforces the main course vibe that comes with this salad. As a comparison, only one salad in France can be considered straight-up masculine and therefore more substantial than *la chèvre chaud*: that is *La Périgourdine* and the duck galore she comes with (*gésier, magret de canard,* foie gras, green beans, and green salad). *La Périgourdine* has obviously lost any connection to femininity.

No Parisian woman could ever order a *Périgourdine.* This is a salad for boys. *La salade de chèvre chaud* is a salad for girls and for girly boys. Much more suited to Paris, really.

USEFUL TIP: At home, just add honey, pepper, and maybe some sesame seeds to look like a superstar chef.

SOUND LIKE A PARISIAN: *Alors, pour moi, le chèvre chaud . . . deux, trois . . . OK, quatre chèvres chauds.* ("So for me, warm goat cheese . . . two, three . . . OK, so four warm goat cheeses.")

100%
PARISIEN
APPROUVÉ

Barack Obama

Most men have qualities and defects. Not Barack Obama. To Parisians, Barack Obama is all qualities. He is the friend, the big brother, the father, and the lover they'd like to have. His deep and reassuring voice, his apparent intelligence and temperance make him the leader Parisians would love for their country.

Over the past twenty years, Paris has massively changed sociologically and therefore politically. The increase in rent and property value has pushed most families and modest households outside the city. The *arrondissements* of the center have turned into a gigantic tourist supermarket with hotels and apartment rentals. The once ghetto *arrondissements* closer to the *péripherique* have been slowly but surely gentrified by a new cast of young professionals identified as *bobos* (*bourgeois bohèmes*). Paris thus shifted from a right-wing city to a left-wing city. Seeing Barack Obama run the United States is therefore a pure delight for these new Parisians. He's left wing enough, but not as backwards as the French left can be (side note: this does not prevent *bobos* from voting for the backwards French Socialist Party—anything that is not right wing is their rule).

Barack Obama's skin color is another element that satisfies Parisians to the highest level. While America has managed to offer the conditions for the establishment of significant African-American middle and upper-middle classes, France has not. Integration of immigrants of African descent into French society is overall quite poor compared to that of other communities. The Parisian *bobo* is not ready to face such a striking reality. Seeing a dark-skinned man access the most powerful position in the world is to him a sign that he is right: there is no problem with immigrants of African origin, since they can even become president of the United States of America. In order to let everyone know how good his heart is, he's always quite prompt to explain that the problem is not culturally a certain category of immigrants but instead and exclusively French society. Racist, oppressive, close-minded French society. A quick look around at that stage might prove him right as indeed, among his friends sitting there listening to him, it will be unlikely to find any dark-skinned people.

Under the governance of George W. Bush, Parisians had extended the scope of their enlightened judgment. France was not the only racist, oppressive, and close-minded country in the world. So was the United States. Today, the Parisian finds himself quite troubled at explaining how Americans managed to elect Barack Obama. In a very Parisian analysis, they will talk about the charisma and charm of the man. But rarely admit the obvious flaws of their previous analysis. Parisians are so scared of coming across as racist that they will adore in a sickly manner any presentable person of African descent. In an ironic whiff of good consciousness, they give kudos to the civilized dark-skinned man. Recent rankings of the most popular people in France have steadily honored French people of African descent (Yannick Noah, Zinédine Zidane, Djamel Debbouze).

In the end, the Parisian is just a dreamer; he would like for his flawed vision of reality to be reality. No matter how off it is, he will use any little hint that could prove him right to support his case. The hope most Parisians share for a French Barack Obama testifies to their same approach to the world. One where constructive pragmatism and hopeful realism don't weigh much faced with dreamy denial and travestied fear.

USEFUL TIP: Sarah Palin? Really?

SOUND LIKE A PARISIAN: *Oh, putain, mais Barack Obama quoi . . . mais quelle classe ce mec: le charisme, élégant, posé. . . . Et puis chapeau quand même.* ("Oh, *putain*, I mean Barack Obama . . . he's in a different league: charisma, intelligence, elegance. . . . Plus I mean congratulations to him.")

Saint-Germain des Prés

Some neighborhoods have it all: the looks, the money, the energy, the legend, and the culture. Saint-Germain des Prés is one of those.

Parisians love to meet up in Saint-Germain for *un ciné à Odéon, un verre rue de Buci, un peu de shopping rue du four, une soirée rue Guisarde* . . . There, Parisians feel like real Parisians, taking full advantage of their Parisianity. Observing and displaying style, sensing civilized crowds, surfing on both the heart and soul of the city. Simply being—in the place to be.

Conveniently enough, the Parisian has changed just as much as Saint-Germain has. The legend of this *quartier* was built over the vibrancy of its intellectual life: Diderot, D'Alembert, Marat, Danton, Boris Vian, Jean-Paul Sartre, Simone de Beauvoir, Godard, Truffaut, Prévert, Giacometti . . . Over the centuries, all these characters made Saint-Germain des Prés the epicenter of a certain Parisian life.

Today, the course of this local history is on hold. Legend and beauty have a value—which is high in a global world. Tourists and *poseurs* have therefore replaced intellectuals, clothing stores opened where bookshops closed, local shop owners sold their leases to big international brands. Saint-Germain has changed. Preserving its beauty but happily stepping on its legend. Everything has its price, and Saint-Germain has cashed in on its.

Yet Parisians are not bitter about it. Most do not even suspect that such changes have happened, and are still happening. They, too, have changed. Entertainment and looks have become more crucial to most Parisians than intellectual life or authenticity. They have grown to understand what money does and to be mostly fine with it.

The Roman Empire thrived on giving its people *panem et circenses* (literally "bread and games"). Our current empire applies the same recipe and keeps its good people in the same felicity. Since Saint-Germain provides excellent *panem* and great *circenses*, it will come as no surprise that all the citizens of the global empire flock to Saint-Germain des Prés to taste its delights.

USEFUL TIP: Pop your collar.

SOUND LIKE A PARISIAN: *On se retrouve à Odéon et on avise.* ("Let's meet up at Odéon and then we'll play it by ear.")

Not Drinking Wine

It is very easy to spot tourists in a Parisian café. They are the ones drinking wine.

The image of wine in France could not be more different from what it is in Anglo countries. There, wine is sophisticated, edgy, cool, sexy, and refined. In Paris, it is just the opposite.

Up until a few years ago, the Parisian associated two mythologies with the concept of wine: on the one hand, wine was very high-end, pricey, and too refined for his palate; on the other, it was somewhere between *le gros rouge qui tâche* and *le petit vin simple*, a drink of little pretension and minimal interest, with a bit of a drunken grandpa's connotation. Most *Parisiens* drank their daily wine as a reflex, for it was simple and very affordable.

But times have changed, as France became the most boringly hygienist country in the world and domestic wine consumption plummeted. The French drink less and less, and the share of wine in their alcohol consumption has eroded significantly to the benefit of beer and spirits (supported by large corporations and excellent marketing and PR strategies—especially compared to those of the French wine industry).

During dinner, younger Parisians do not opt for wine automatically. Water, beer, and cocktails are serious rivals (water having no rival at lunchtime). To relax, most opt for beer or coffee, except in the summer when they might go *rosé.* Close intimacy between young Parisians and their beer shows in that they have nicknames for it: *une bière* will usually be called *une binch, une binouze*, or *une mousse*. Brands of beer even have their nicknames ("16" for 1664, "Kro" for Kronenbourg). Ironically enough, the same pattern can be witnessed in Anglo countries, but with wine ("vino," "cab," "chard," "sauv blanc," "Two-Buck Chuck"). To party in Paris, wine is simply out of the question: party is about gin, vodka, and whiskey. At home, very few Parisians will pop a bottle of wine open after a long day at work. Pastis or whiskey is usually the drink of choice for the Parisian's homey *apéro*. Wine all in all is left alone by younger Parisians: ostracized.

The category of people that turn their back to wine in the most blatant manner is not younger Parisians though. It is Parisian women. Wine, being alcohol, has two main characteristics: it makes you fat and it makes you lose control. There are no reasons to drink wine. Whatsoever. The only wine *la Parisienne* can tolerate is champagne. *Bien frais s'il vous plait.* Frequently sweetened and colored up a bit as it gets turned into a Kir Royal. After two sips, *la Parisienne* will claim that she's tipsy and shut down for the rest of the evening, secretly blaming the person in front of her for making her drink.

Recently, the edgiest *bobos* have started to frequent the few wine bars that specialize in *vins naturels*, which have flourished over the past few years. *Vins naturels* is an interesting concept of a category of wines made with very little, if any, sulfites. Most of these wines are bad, with striking technical defects, and fully overpriced. They are presented as wines with great personality to gullible and self-absorbed *bobos* who believe that because these wines are *naturel*, they are "real." And that, consequently, all other wines are not.

Between Parisians who are not really drinking wine, those drinking not real wine, and those drinking what they're sure is real wine, the Parisian wine situation is quite disconcerting. Only one thing is certain: Parisians should drink more if it.

USEFUL TIP: For an exciting wine experience in Paris (there is nothing wrong with a shameless plug), sign up for one of Ô Chateau's wine tastings on www.o-chateau.com. They are informative and fun. Also, for good wines in a great environment in Paris (including many legendary French wines by the glass), come to my wine bar: 68, rue Jean-Jacques Rousseau in the 1st *arrondissement*. And be prepared to have some fun. Some of us Parisians resist.

SOUND LIKE A PARISIAN: *Tu veux du vin? Non? OK. Non, merci, une carafe d'eau s'il vous plait.* ("Would you like some wine? No? OK. No thank you, just a carafe of water, please.")

100%